Passages: A Collection of Personal Histories
of Chippiannock Cemetery
Edited by Terri Wiebenga

Copyright © 2006
Chippiannock Cemetery Heritage Foundation
All rights reserved. No part of this book may be
reproduced in any means, print or electronic,
without consent of:
Chippiannock Cemetery Heritage Foundation
2901 12th Street
Rock Island IL 61201

 THIS BOOK IS MADE POSSIBLE IN
PART BY A GRANT FROM THE
ILLINOIS HUMANITIES COUNCIL,
the National Endowment for the Humanities, and the Illinois
General Assembly. The views expressed herein do not necessarily
represent those of the Illinois Humanities Council or the National
Endowment for the Humanities, or the Illinois General Assembly.

Razor Edge Press
PO Box 1412
Bettendorf, Iowa 52722

ISBN 978-0-9774018-1-9
Library of Congress Control Number: 2006933315
Printed in the United States of America by
Lightning Source, LaVergne, Tennessee

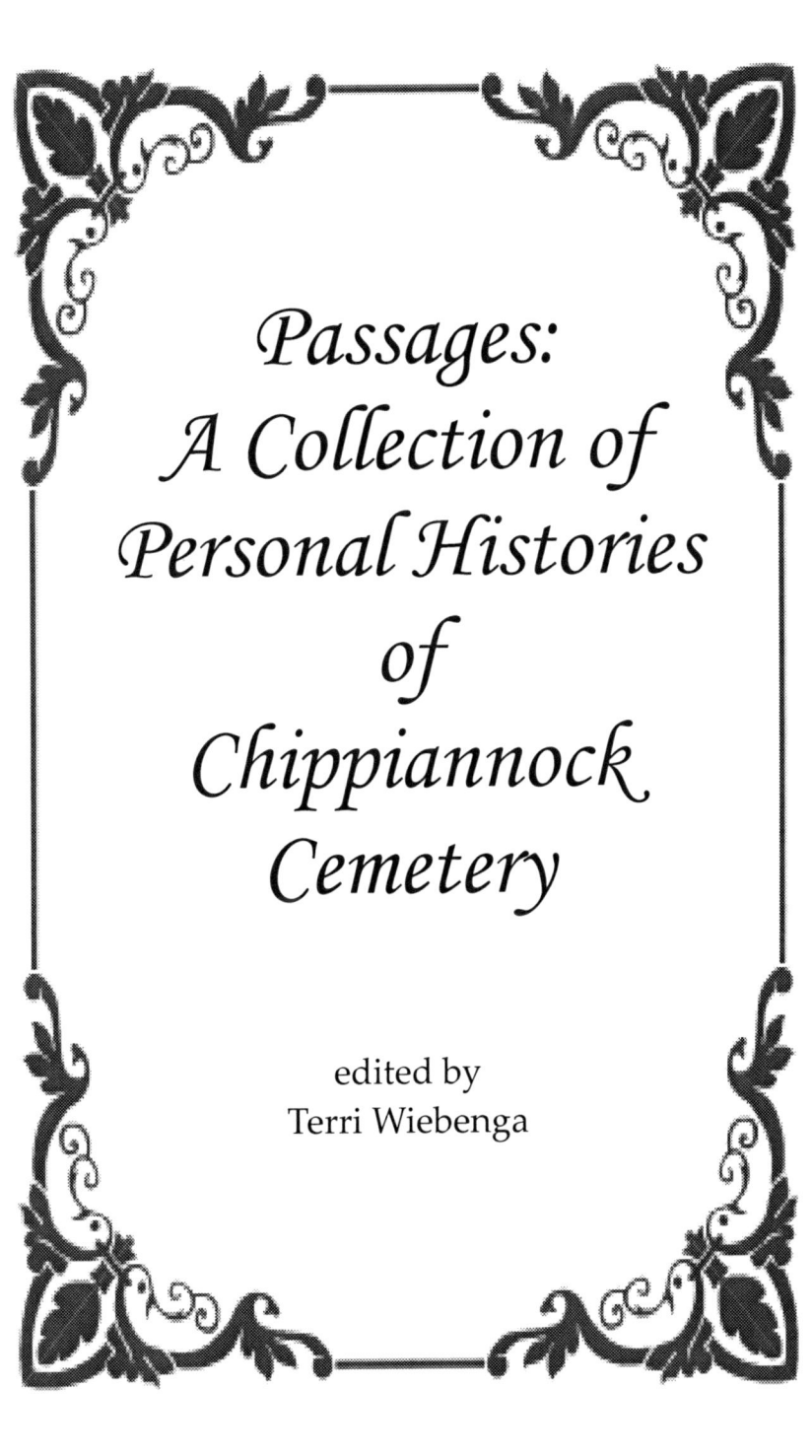

Passages:
A Collection of Personal Histories of Chippiannock Cemetery

edited by
Terri Wiebenga

Acknowledgements

Thank you to Greg Vogele and Tracey McVay at the Chippiannock Cemetery office for their efficiency and diligence; Jill Doak for her grant-writing and her historical knowledge; Bj Elsner for agreeing to serve as Grant Evaluator and for her proof-reading skills; and the people all over the country who agreed to share the stories of their ancestors with us. Use of the book, *Rock Island: Yesterday, Today & Tomorrow,* edited by Bj Elsner, was invaluable.

Special thanks to Bruce Walters for offering the use of his beautiful drawings:

Winter (detail)	cover
Cable Monument	cover
Winter	page 1
Hallowed Ground	page 55
Lachesis	page 125

Note:
People mentioned in this book who are buried at Chippiannock have a parenthetical notation after their names stating their years of birth and death. If they plan to be buried at Chippiannock but are still living, only the birth date appears.

Table of Contents

Individuals

Edward Bauersfeld 3
Margaret Cheney.. 7
Thomas Cheney.. 9
Johnny Ellis 13
Kermit Hotvedt 15
Caleb Langston... 19
Leonard Meyers.. 23
Isaiah Nelson 27
Frank and Cameron Palicki 29
John Schneider... 33
Lloyd Schwiebert 35
Charles Spaulding.. 39
Richard Swanson... 43
Joseph Vogele 47
Jack Vukov 51

Families

Ainsworth/Cook 57

Aster/Hartz/Simmon/Wilson/Colburn 61

Cleaveland/Hayes 65

Dingeldein 69

Downing 73

Ferguson/Bleuer/Lamp 79

Franing/Bendt/Andrews 85

Gitt/Ailes/Berg/Skarp 91

Herrmann 99

Schneider/Wieland/Foley 103

Tanner/Means/Bowen/Dickinson 109

Weckel/Bollinger/Erickson/Jackson 115

Wood 121

Notables

Felicia Buford	127
Napoleon Bonaparte Buford	131
Jonah H. Case	135
Bailey Davenport	139
Susan Lewis Goldsmith	143
Samuel S. Guyer	147
Holmes Hakes	151
Ben Harper	155
Charles Bishop Knox	159
Isaac Negus	163
Marcus Brutus Osborn	167
Morris Rosenfield	171
Leopold Simon	175
Mary Hall Wadsworth	177

Photographs and Illustrations

Winter 1
Edward Bauersfeld 3
Margaret and Thomas Cheney 8
Johnny Ellis 13
Kermit Hotvedt 15
Caleb Langston 19
Leonard Meyers 23
Isaiah Nelson 27
Frank and Cameron Palicki 29
Lloyd Schwiebert 35
Charles Spaulding 39
Richard Swanson 43
Joseph Vogele 47
Jack Vukov 51
Hallowed Ground 55
Ainsworth family headstone 57
Aster family headstone 61
Emma Aster and Ben C. Hartz headstones 62
Colburn family headstone 64
Cleaveland family headstone 65
Olivia Hayes Cleaveland 67
Henry C. Cleaveland 67

Philip Dingeldein	69
Philip Dingeldein, Sr.	70
Philip Dingeldein, Jr.	71
Jane York Downing	73
George C. Downing	73
Jennie Downing	74
John Downing	76
Bleuer's Band	79
Benjamin and Rose Lemberg Bleuer	81
Anna Caldwell Franing	85
Russell Lowell Lawson Franing	87
C. Lewis Franing headstone	89
Jacob and Nannie Ailes Gitt	91
Gustaf and Maydie Gitt Berg	93
Carl Knute Berg	94
Andreas Hermann	99
Regula Rissi Herrmann	99
Henry and Andreas Herrmann	100
Grey Eagle pitcher	104
Grey Eagle pitcher spout detail	107
Gilbert and Henrietta Bowen family	111
Esther Bowen Tanner, Esther Tanner Means, and Marion Esther Means	113
John and Eva Weckel Bollinger	116

Thomas M. Jackson 119
Adolph Weckel descendants —
    three generations 120
Wood family headstone 121
Lachesis 125
James and Felicia Buford headstone 127
Col. John and N. B. Buford headstone 131
Case family headstone 135
Davenport family and B.D. headstones 139
Davenport family and Mother
    (Susan Goldsmith) headstones 143
Guyer family headstone 147
Hakes family headstone 151
Harper family headstone 155
Knox family headstone 159
Negus family headstone 163
Marcus Osborn headstone 167
Rosenfield family headstone 171
Leopold Simon headstone 175
Mitchell family headstone 177
Mary Wadsworth headstone 180

Individuals

—Bruce Walters

Edward Bauersfeld
1862–1925

Edward was born Aug. 10, 1862, in Buffalo New York, and moved to Rock Island when he was a child with his parents John (1814–1884) and Johanna (1819–1895), four sisters, and one brother, William (1852–1836). He was educated in the local German Lutheran and public schools, and completed a night school business course at Rock Island High School.

In his first job, he was employed as a tinner, and then spent a number of years working in the railroad shops in Davenport, Iowa. In 1898 he and M.H. Sexton started a laundry business—Rock Island Steam Laundry. Edward was active in management of that business for over 30 years.

On June 17, 1894, he married Magdalene (Lena) Fluegel (1871–1944) of Rock Island. She was the daughter of K. Henry Fluegel (1838–1911) and A. Margaretha Fluegel (1837–1914), who emigrated from Bavaria, Germany, when Lena was two years old.

Edward and Lena had one daughter, Ada, and two sons, Roy Edward (1901–1914) and Frank Edward (1892–1976).

When Roy was 13 years old, he drowned in the back waters of the river. This affected the family for years, and Edward carried a picture of Roy in his pocket watch all his life.

Politically, Edward was a faithful Democrat. His first act of public service was as Rock Island township collector. In 1916 and 1917 he served as a supervisor on the Rock Island County Board. From 1919 to 1922 he was a member of the Rock Island police and fire commission under Mayor Harry Schriver. This was during Schriver's second term in office, after he had run the notorious gangster John Looney out of town.

Like most businessmen of the time, Edward was active in many community organizations. He was a member of the Modern Woodmen of America and the Rock Island Elks Lodge No. 980.

During the days of Three-I League baseball in Rock Island, he acted as president of the local baseball club for many years. The Illinois-Indiana-Iowa League (also known as the "Three-I" or "3-Eye") was a national force in minor league baseball for the first sixty years of the 20th century. Edward's son, Frank, was instrumental in bringing the Three-I League to Rock Island. Frank also organized and managed the Rock Island All-Stars baseball team and played semi-pro baseball in Geneseo, Illinois.

In the spring of 1925, an ailing Edward spent six weeks in Hot Springs, Arkansas, attempting to regain his health. Three weeks later, on May 4, 1925, he died at his home.

Frank married Dorothy May Dailey (1894–1964), daughter of John C. Dailey (1867–1943) and Ida Randbarger (1872–1931). Her great-grandparents were among the first settlers in Rock Island County in 1837, and her ancestor, John Dailey, came to America in 1662, dying in Providence, Rhode Island in 1720. Dorothy's sisters were Mary (1896–1988)—a school teacher for 45 years; Ruth (1901–1979)—also a school teacher for 30 years; and Grace (1905–1948)—a stenographer for the Corps of Engineers on Rock Island Arsenal.

Frank and Dorothy had two children, John and Richard. John Edward Sr. married Kathryn Erwin and they had three children, John Jr., Edward, named after his ancestor, and Nancy. Richard (1926) married Eileen Reinhart (1927–2000) and they had one child, Kathleen Mary Opler, who now lives in Bellevue, Washington.

The Rock Island Steam Laundry continued to be owned and operated by the Bauersfeld family until 1989. It missed being a century family business by only a few years. Edward's descendents still live in Rock Island, representing five generations of Bauersfelds. Some are or have been 50-year members of various local organizations and have served in elected or appointed positions, just like their active ancestor.

—submitted by Richard Dailey Bauersfeld

Margaret P. Cheney
1915–2004

Margaret was born July 15, 1915, in Rushville, Nebraska, daughter of Charles and Alice Hitchens Phillippe. She had one brother. Margaret graduated in 1937 from the University of Nebraska, Lincoln, with a major in music. While attending college, she was a member of Alpha Omicron Pi sorority, Sigma Alpha Iota music sorority and Mortar Board. She taught music at Unadilla (Nebraska) High School until marrying Thomas W. Cheney on October 15, 1938, in Lincoln, Nebraska.

Margaret and Tom went on to have one daughter, Patricia, and one son, Thomas C. Their daughter married Larry Keim and moved to Goldsboro, North Carolina. Their son Thomas C. and his wife Eileen live in Lewes, Delaware. Margaret's grandchildren are Steven Keim, Marsha Keim Ollie, John Keim, Matthew Cheney, and Brian Cheney. Her great-grandchildren are Isabelle Keim, Olivia Keim, Rose Cheney, Kate Cheney, Nathaniel Cheney, Leah Ollie, and William Cheney.

Margaret served as an elder and deacon in the South Park Presbyterian Church in Rock Island, Illinois. She also sang in the choir and taught a women's Bible class for over 30 years. She was a member and past president of Chapter BK of the PEO Sisterhood, a philanthropic organization where women celebrate, educate, and motivate other women to achieve their goals. Activities in support of her community included serving on the board of directors of the former Huber Home, Franciscan Hospital Auxiliary, YWCA, and Marriage and Family Counseling Service. Her grass roots service included delivering Meals on Wheels, volunteering for *The Argus* Santa, and working at the Quad City Open.

When not serving one of her many philanthropic causes, Margaret could often be found at the Rock Island Arsenal Golf Club, playing bridge or golfing. She was also an excellent fisherwoman and enjoyed traveling all over the world with her husband, Tom.

Margaret P. Cheney, 88, of Rock Island, died Thursday, Feb. 5, 2004, at her home. She was dearly loved and cherished by her family and leaves a great legacy of love and community service.

Thomas W. Cheney
1914–2004

Thomas was born in Union, Nebraska, on December 17, 1914, to G. Ward and Vernie Barnum Cheney, who also had two daughters. While attending the University of Nebraska at Lincoln, Tom joined Modern Woodmen of America, a fraternal life insurance society. In 1936, he graduated with a Bachelor of Science Degree in Business Administration, and on October 15, 1938, he married Margaret Phillippe. He then worked for Modern Woodmen's Home Office Agency Department in Rock Island, Illinois, until joining the United States Air Corps in 1941.

Tom spent a year serving as an officer in the primary training school at Cimarron Field in Oklahoma City, Oklahoma, before being assigned to glider school at Goodland, Kansas. He then spent a six month stint as college student recruiter. In July 1943, he attended the Command and General Staff School at Fort Leavenworth, Kansas. After graduating in September, he joined the 475th Fighter Group in New Guinea, where he served as the executive officer.

A month later he was sent with General McArthur to the Philippines, participating in the occupation of that country for almost two years. During this period, Tom was promoted to Lieutenant Colonel and was privileged to witness General McArthur signing the peace treaty with Japan at Ei Shima. During the five years he served his country, Tom was awarded the Legion of Merit, a Presidential Unit Citation, and four major battle stars.

After returning home in December 1945, he resumed his job at Modern Woodmen's Home Office in Rock Island, before being appointed Manager of the Society's Oklahoma agency. Tom rose quickly through the company's ranks, being elected to the Board of Directors in February 1954 and appointed Assistant to the President in September 1954. He was named President of Modern Woodmen in January 1960 and served in that capacity for 19½ years before retiring in 1979.

During his tenure as president, the current seven-story office building was built in 1967 at a cost of seven million. Under his dedicated leadership the company experienced record growth. He was considered a mentor, a gentleman, and a well-respected and well-regarded businessman by his colleagues and the community.

Tom's business acumen was also recognized on a national level. He served as president of the National Fraternal Congress of America, appeared in "Who's Who in America", "Who's Who in Business and Industry", and "Who's Who in Insurance."

Statewide, he was Director and Vice Chairman of the Illinois State Chamber of Commerce, and served 12 years on the Advisory Committee to the College of Commerce and Business Administration of the University of Illinois.

Within the community, he was a president of the Rock Island Chamber of Commerce and Junior

Chamber of Commerce, chairman of the Quad City Council of Commerce Presidents, a charter member and on the Board of Trustees at Franciscan Medical Center and the Trinity Health Foundation Board. He served as president of the Board of Governors of Franciscan Hospital and was a member of the Board of Governors of the former St. Anthony's Hospital.

In addition, Tom served on the board of directors of the Rock Island City and County Community Chests, the Rock Island YMCA and Augustana College. Tom sat on the board of directors and executive committee of the First National Bank of the Quad Cities for 13 years. He was also a former member of the Board of Governors and past president of the Rock Island Arsenal Golf Club. He was an active member in the South Park Presbyterian Church of Rock Island, serving as deacon, trustee, and elder, and chairing several internal committees over the years.

Thomas W. Cheney, died Tuesday, Nov. 30, 2004, at age 89. He will long be remembered as a man who supported his family, served his community, and helped build the foundation of one of the country's leading fraternal insurance societies.

—submitted by Thomas C. Cheney, the son of Margaret and Thomas W. Cheney

Johnny L. Ellis
1949–2005

Johnny was born on October 19, 1949, in Mississippi and moved with his family to Rock Island at age 4. He attended Rock Island schools, Southern Illinois University and Western Illinois University. He met Anita Triplett in 1982, and they got married in 1992. He had six brothers, one sister, one son, one daughter, five grandchildren, one stepson, one step-grandchild, and many nieces and nephews.

Johnny was a staunch politician. In 1990, he was elected Precinct Committeeman for Rock Island Ward 32, and was elected to the Rock Island County Board in 1996. His focus was always on community activism. He was instrumental in getting a medical clinic established on 11th Street. Until then, low income people from Rock Island had to walk to the Community Health Center in Davenport, Iowa. He provided assistance to the elderly and handicapped, and compared himself favorably to the famous attorney Johnnie Cochran. His unfulfilled dream was to hold statewide office.

Johnny also cared for the youth of his community. He greatly admired Harry Pells—former general manager of the Quad City Angels and assistant coach of the Augustana baseball team—and served as a Little League coach. At his death, he was working on the establishment of a youth cultural center in Rock Island.

Another community project he didn't live to finish was the concept of rest areas and business growth along 11th Street. He thought this neglected area could be a vital social and economic part of the city, since it is connected with highways at both ends and serves as a major thoroughfare through Rock Island.

As a teenager, Johnny had no direction and ended up serving time in more than one correctional institution. Through self-discipline, he raised himself out of those negative behaviors, and chose to give to the community what he felt he had taken from it. He was employed as a GED instructor at Scott Community College, and with the Rock Island Park District. He enjoyed reading and writing and loved teaching people how to read.

Johnny Ellis died on October 17, 2005, and is buried near his father and two of his brothers. Anita feels lucky to have married a man with such foresight and vision for his community, and is trying to carry on his good works.

—submitted by his wife, Anita Ellis

Kermit O. Hotvedt
1914–2005

In 1852, the Hotvedt family immigrated to Decorah, a Norwegian community. Kermit was born on December 27, 1914, in Chester, Iowa, on the farm of his mother's family (Ole and Anna Goodwin Juve). His brother Alton was born in 1912 and his sister Alice in 1919. Their family lived near Luther College, but farmed 70-80 acres outside of town, close by to many relatives. The Lutheran Church played an important part in their family life, with church activities being the focus of their social gatherings.

Kermit was a lifeguard at the newly opened Decorah City Municipal Pool, and, like Ronald Reagan, he helped save the lives of many. In summer 1933, after high school graduation, he attended the Citizens' Military Training Camps in Fort Des Moines, Iowa, where he earned status as Expert Rifleman and was recommended for appointment in the Officers' Reserve Corps

While attending Luther College he was a member of the Turning Team (gymnastics) and a member of the Letterman's Club. He graduated in 1938 with a BA in economics and science, and first taught general science at a junior high school in Blue Earth, Minnesota. He joined the Navy in 1941 and was sent to Flight Training in Minneapolis, then to Florida. In December of 1941 he graduated from the Pensacola Aviation Cadet Regiment at the top of the class and remained there as a PBY Flight Instructor.

In 1943, while still at Pensacola NAS, he met and married a Rock Island girl whose father was also stationed there. Barbara Sala (1924–1982) was the daughter of Margaret (nee Anderson) and Roland O. Sala. Dr. Sala, whose family owned the Sala apartment buildings, was the youngest of five generations of Sala doctors and he tended patients in Rock Island for many years. Margaret Anderson (1898–1982) was the daughter of K.T. Anderson (1869-1959), who served as Vice President of First National Bank, and Netta Bartholomew Anderson. Netta (1873–1960) was the daughter of Edward Fry Bartholomew (1846–1946), former President of Carthage College, Carthage, Illinois, and beloved professor of religion and philosophy at Augustana College for 41 years until age 82.

In 1944, Kermit began flying night missions in the Pacific, conducting anti-sub warfare and protecting the invading U.S. fleet around Saipan, Tinian, and Guam. When he returned home at Christmas, he found out that he had a new baby daughter, Lynne. He and Barbara would go on to have two more daughters, Susan and Katherine. He finished his next tour of duty patrolling the Atlantic, and after the end of World War II, he remained in the Naval Reserves for 16 years.

The family lived in Rock Island, Illinois, while the daughters were growing up. When he came back from the war it was difficult finding a job that would make him feel fulfilled. He tried various fields, at one point owning a small family grocery and serving as the principal of Barstow School, a small country school not far from Rock Island. But it was at Rock Island Lincoln School that he really hit his stride, teaching physical education, health, and science. All three of his daughters had him as their teacher and walked to school with him in the mornings. Teaching was his gift and at every opportunity, he taught his family and students without preaching.

After years of searching for the perfect property, Kermit and Barbara built a summer home on a lovely private lake in Wisconsin, board by board, brick by brick. It was here that they came together in the later years for family reunions, vacations, solace. Grandchildren came along and they too loved the woodlands and the ones who inhabited it. Even at 85, Kermit was still rowing and swimming around the perimeter of the lake for exercise.

He began competing in the Master's Swimming Program with the Rock Island YMCA, and when Barbara died, he practiced even harder. At his first National Masters Swim he met Win Kennedy, a woman who loved swimming as much as he did. They married, and together they competed in international and national swim meets with the St. Pete Masters, near their home in St. Petersburg, Florida, and won almost every event they entered.

Kermit Hotvedt was a hero to the men he flew with in World War II, to the people who knew him as an All American swimmer, and most of all, to his daughters.

He was admired and respected by all who knew him, and had a great sense of humor. He was modest about his accomplishments, yet his accomplishments were many.

He was a remarkable man. I am proud to be his daughter!

—submitted by Lynne Schrom

Caleb B. Langston
1920–1997

Caleb was born in Matherville, Illinois, on September 6, 1920, the son of Thomas James Langston and Mary Jane Purvis Langston. Thomas worked in the coal mines in Matherville while Mary Jane helped her mother, Mary Jane Sutherland Purvis, to run a boarding house for miners. The family moved to Rock Island in 1920. Caleb went to school at the old Hawthorne School and later to Grant School, and finally to the old Rock Island High School on 21st Street.

Caleb joined the Civilian Conservation Corps in 1938 and was sent to Wyoming where he enjoyed the rugged life and often spoke of the magnificent views to be seen there. He returned home to Rock Island in 1942 and in June of that year, he joined the Army. He was then sent to boot camp at Fort Bragg at Charlotte, North Carolina. After completing his training he was chosen to serve in the Military Police and sent to Camp Riley in Minnesota. Christmas of that year found him at Camp Lockborne in Ohio and he often told of watching Bob Hope's Christmas show there when the orders came for his unit to go overseas. The show was interrupted as his group filed out.

In January 1943, he crossed the Atlantic on board the Queen Mary, docking at Glasgow, Scotland. Caleb was assigned to the Headquarters of the Eighth Army Air Corps at Huntingdon, England. About a year later he was moved to the town of Wellingborough, England, where he met his wife Pamela M. Sanders. They were married on Monday, February 12, 1945, at the Church of Our Lady in Wellingborough. The day after the wedding he was shipped out to Maastricht in the Netherlands. From there his unit moved into Germany and was with the American troops that liberated the infamous concentration camp at Dachau. Caleb was finally stationed at Munich until the end of the war. Caleb returned to the United Sates in November 1945.

He then began work as a clerk on the Rock Island Lines. His wife came to Rock Island in May 1946. Caleb and Pamela had three children, Bruce, Gregory, and Elaine. Caleb also worked as a manager for the Thom McAn shoe store in Rock Island and for a time as a salesman for State Farm Insurance. He returned to the railroad but after the demise of the Rock Island Lines, he went to work as a car upholsterer at Glass Service Center in Rock Island, which he retired from in 1985.

Caleb was an avid bowler and once bowled a 300 game. In 1961 he won the Rock Island Men's Singles championship. He bowled regularly with several leagues and competed in many tournaments each year. He also enjoyed playing golf with his friends and after he retired he played many times each week. In his lifetime he had three holes-in-one, one at Indian Bluff and two at Saukie Golf Course. He also enjoyed classical music, especially the works of Mozart and operas. He was an avid reader of non-fiction with his special interest being the Civil War and books about the Lincoln era.

Caleb dearly loved his family. He always had time to attend their school programs and sporting events. It was his great joy to take his children to the bowling alley, and later to teach them to play golf. In later life his great love was his grandchildren.

Caleb became ill in 1996 and gradually lost the ability to bowl and to play golf and to do all the other things that he enjoyed. When he died on September 17, 1997, he left a great void in his family never to be filled. The devastation of the loss of this unselfish, genial and benevolent man will remain as long as our memory of him endures.

—submitted by his wife, Pamela Langston

Leonard Meyers
1927–1995

Leonard was born March 6, 1927, in Rock Island, in the family home which was next to a chicken hatchery. His father, Walter Barrett Meyers, was the son of George Washington and Jennie Barrett Meyers, who had one other son, Charles. Leonard's great-great-grandmother was Cherokee. Leonard's mother was Lula Schmid, the daughter of Gottlieb and Regina Schmidt (aka Schmid). Lula had seven sisters, Mary, Emma, Ida, Rose, Lilly, Regina, Frances, and three brothers, John, Herman and Raymond.

Lenny was educated in the local public school system and graduated from Rock Island High. He had four sisters, Jennie, Lila, Carol, and Frances Marie, and four brothers, Walt, Ray, Earl, and Jimmy. Frances Marie (1921) died before age one and is buried next to Lenny.

He got polio at the age of 3½ and was paralyzed from head to toe. His mother would have to close his eyes for him at night and open them in the morning. He couldn't swallow, so they would hold him up with a hand on his back and a hand on his stomach, then put soft food in his mouth and rock him back and forth until it went down his throat. After several months it cleared up and only affected his left arm permanently, which was caused by a complete body cast that raised his left arm to shoulder height.

From ages 12 to 18 he had five surgeries to regain some use of his left arm and fingers. He thought his dad was the meanest man on earth because he wouldn't let his mom tie his shoes for him. Later he realized his dad was making him independent so that he would know that he could do anything anyone else could do, and was always grateful to his dad for that.

While in elementary school, he traveled for two summers with Honest Bert's Wonder Show, living in the Fat Lady's wagon. At each town he would don a cowboy outfit and ride around a pony that sported a banner advertising the circus. As a teenager, he worked for a riding stable in Milan, leading trail rides from 6 a.m. until midnight, 7 days a week. He discovered he didn't like to participate in rodeo, but won several ribbons showing horses and riding in the Quad City area parades.

He worked at Bertman Electric Co. as a welder and spray painter during the day, and was an auto mechanic at night. Next he carried air mail during the day, and at night ran a wrecker service and operated a crane with Jack Penny. He then worked at Wilkins Pipe & Supply Co. as assistant warehouse foreman. His last job was at Flicks as manager of the warehouse.

He married Rhoda Mae Bjorkman on July 15, 1949. They had a son, Lyle Lee, whom Lenny was very proud of. Lyle joined the Navy, became a nurse and retired as Captain from the Rock Island Fire Department in 2005. Their daughter Linda Louise is a social worker. He had three grandchildren: Andy Anderson, Amanda Meyers, and Stephen Meyers. He loved them very much and enjoyed spending time with them. He said that the only thing wrong with being a grandpa was that meant he was sleeping with a grandma!

In the more than 46 years they were married, life was never dull. He loved to bring home animals: 12 baby ducks, newborn kittens whose mother had been killed, a nanny goat, two young mares, and a pair of Mexican burros, just to mention a few.

They enjoyed the winter of 1994–95 in Florida in a motor home. He died Sept. 22, 1995, of lung cancer. He was loved by everyone who met him. He was very outgoing and always willing to help in any way he could.

—submitted by his wife, Rhoda Meyers

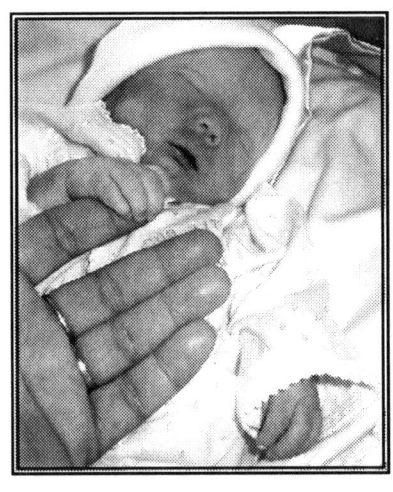

Isaiah Nelson
April 23, 2004

Isaiah Kenneth Cory Nelson was born on April 23, 2004, at 8:21 a.m. and lived for 47 glorious minutes. While *in utero*, he was diagnosed with bilateral renal agensis, a chromosome disorder. Although he wasn't due until Memorial Day, he was delivered at 35 weeks gestation, since it was likely he would be stillborn if he was carried to full term.

While Isaiah was alive he blinked once, but did not cry. He was baptized and was welcomed by many of his relatives and others who love him, including his Mommy—Tina, his Daddy—Kenneth, his brother—Brandon, and his sister—Lilllie.

Like her little brother, Lillie was a miracle birth. Although she was born with the same chromosome disorder and was not expected to live a full year, she is now five years old. She has had five surgeries, has a gastrointestinal tube, suffers from Cerebral Palsy, is non-verbal, has seizures, and wears bilateral hearing aids, but she is a happy little girl.

The Nelson family prepared two keepsake albums of Isaiah. These contain photos of his birth, his time here on earth, graveside services, monument, and family members. It also contains his birth and death certificates, obituary, notes from caring friends and strangers, and other mementoes. These albums are precious keepsakes; however, the true memory of Isaiah lives in the hearts of all those whose lives he touched.

Family members who repose with Isaiah at Chippiannock are Otis Myers—his great-grandfather, Michael Poe, Jr.—his second cousin, and McKenzie Kent—his fourth cousin.

> Our Sweet Baby Angel Isaiah
> our time with you was so brief
> but we are so thankful
> for the time God granted us.
> Daddy, Mommy, Brother and Sister,
> will forever cherish every second
> we had with you.
> We know that you are
> with the Lord
> and that helps us
> to find some comfort
> in our broken hearts.
> You have touched so many lives
> you will never be forgotten.
> You will be missed dearly with
> every breath we take.
> Isaiah you are
> and will always be
> our precious Angel.
>   —written with love by your Mommy. I miss you.

Frank Edward and Cameron Mary Palicki

Frank is a native of the Quad Cities, born and raised in Moline. Cameron's childhood home is northwest Iowa. The two met in Des Moines, Iowa, at Drake University. Frank graduated from Drake in the School of Pharmacy, and has practiced pharmacy for more than forty years. Cameron completed a two-year course in Secretarial Science at Drake and then married Frank. After his graduation, they moved to Rock Island. Frank worked for the old Schlegel Drug Store in East Moline. Cameron worked as a secretary in the law firm of Moran, Klochau, McCarthy & Johnson in Rock Island.

In 1961 they bought the old Johnson Drug Store in Milan, Illinois, and the family moved to Milan and purchased a home there. They raised four children, three girls and a boy. Their children are: Deborah Jo, Elizabeth Anne, Mary Kay, and David Eric. For twenty years, the family lived in Milan, later building a home in the wooded Matthew Heights addition. Cameron stayed at home with the children for many years.

Frank later sold the store and worked for several chain stores, including K-Mart and Shop-Ko. He presently is employed at a Rock Island Walgreens store. Cameron worked for 20 years at Friendship Manor in Rock Island, and part-time at the American Bank & Trust in Rock Island. The family has membership at St. James Lutheran Church in Rock Island.

Frank and Cam have eight grandchildren and two step-grandchildren, which they enjoy as often as they can. Frank loves to hunt and fish and Cam enjoys reading, cooking and walking. They went to Europe in the spring of 2003 and it was the trip of a lifetime.

Frank's dad took him fishing when he was a little boy. He remembers riding on the city bus to the Rock River near Milan and fishing all day, then riding home on a later bus. Years later, they fished in the backwaters of the Mississippi in Mercer County, his mother's original home, where he learned to love the sport.

Frank enjoys hunting deer with his son and hunting ducks with friends. Back in the days when birds were plentiful, Frank hunted pheasant and quail with his own hunting dogs, an Irish Setter named Lucky and an English Setter named Mike. Cam had learned to prepare game when she was a girl in northwest Iowa, where her dad used to find excellent pheasant and duck hunting.

Cam's passion is traveling, and the trip to Europe just whetted her appetite. She and Frank have been to most of the continental United States, Mexico and Canada. Cam's brother, Grant, lives in Seattle, Washington, so that is another place they visit. The family enjoyed fishing in the Sioux Narrows area of Lake of the Woods in Canada several years.

Recently they discovered Chippiannock Cemetery and have a favorite area where they walk almost every day with their little dog, Max. They love it here and are happy to have decided that it shall be the final resting place for two outdoor-lovers.

—submitted by Frank and Cam Palicki

John Andrew James Schneider
1951–

My life as John Andrew James Schneider started the morning of August 17, 1951, in Streator, Illinois. My family consisted of my mother, Josephine Ann Gaydos, my father, Warren Robert Schneider, and my older brother Pete.

Small town life was great. I felt safe and secure walking down streets day or night. I was not the best at school until seventh and eighth grades, when my teachers created a love of knowledge. This love of knowledge led to a degree in teaching from Eastern Illinois University.

God has touched and guided my life. I have been very fortunate coming from hard-working, solid parents. Fate allowed me to have the job of teaching for more than 30 years. The memories, good and bad, are too numerous to reflect on here.

Love found, love lost was my first marriage to Margaret Holland. We waited seven years before Eric Jon was born. Jack Robert came to us two years later. After a separation in 1991 things were not the same even though we got back together. Then in 1995 after 21 years of marriage, the divorce came.

Coaching football, track and soccer has also rewarded me in many ways! It is just another form of teaching. I would like to think I have been good at it. I also worked part time so my family could have the things they needed. One of those places was A-1 Rental, where I worked for 20 summers and almost every Saturday.

One of my part time jobs led to my soul mate. My friend Sheri from Toys R Us asked me if I wanted to start dating again. I didn't think I was ready, but she convinced me to call Susan Kay Tobin. We met and talked a lot. She was a mother of a young boy, Adam. From the first kiss, which almost made me lose my gum, our love has grown. I wish that I would have had more time with you, Susan.

After two years we married. Adam asked me to adopt him, which made me proud. I hope he never regrets it. Adam Lee Pete Schneider is his adoptive name. Then our lives were given Blake Andrew in 1998. Four boys! They never will understand until they have children.

Husband, son, father, teacher, coach, and Christian is what I have been. "Gladly would he learn and gladly teach." God forgive me.

—submitted by John Schneider

Lloyd A. Schwiebert
1913–2004

Lloyd Alvin Rudolph Schwiebert was born on June 6, 1913, in Moline, Illinois, of immigrant parents, William R. Schwiebert and Anna Lührs Schwiebert. William and Anna had immigrated to the United States in the early 20th Century. William worked as a machinist for International Harvester, Midland, Automobile, and finally, beginning in 1914, at the Rock Island Arsenal, where he advanced through a series of promotions until retirement in 1947.

The Schwiebert household, like many immigrant households, though not wealthy in material goods, was filled with love. William provided the "tough love" of a rather stern, hard working, and thrifty father, determined to make a better life for his family in their new homeland. Anna provided encouragement and nurture to Lloyd and his older brother, Paul, as well as Margaret Ann, who arrived in 1926.

Lloyd attended public schools in Moline and in 1931, graduated from Moline High School, where he participated in speech and drama clubs as well as band.

One of the greatest influences on Lloyd's life came from his brother Paul, who sacrificed by postponing his own graduate education to help Lloyd finance his education. At Augustana College in Rock Island, Illinois, Lloyd excelled in oratory and graduated in just three years. He then attended the University of Iowa Law School, where he was honored to be named co-editor of the Law Review his senior year.

Upon being admitted to the Bar, Lloyd practiced briefly in Davenport, Iowa, before setting up an office in Moline. He worked mostly as a solo practitioner until 1975, when his son, Mark, joined the practice. Over the years, Lloyd became a highly-regarded family lawyer and served on many local Bar committees and activities, and on a state board that oversaw the ethical practice of law.

Lloyd also gave generously of his time to civic and church organizations. He was active in Luther League, served on Augustana College Board of Directors and the Moline School Board, was President of the Board of Directors of the Lutheran Hospital in Moline and President of the Augustana Brotherhood, and was one of the founders of the Augustana Research Foundation, which he helped direct for over 50 years,

Lloyd married Olive E. Johnson, then Dean of Women at Augustana College, in 1947. Their marriage lasted for more than 55 years, producing four children: Lloyd Peter, a physician and professor of Family Medicine at the University of Oklahoma and medical textbook author; Mark, an attorney who practiced law with Lloyd for over 25 years and served as Mayor of the

City of Rock Island for many years; Sara, a not-for-profit organization executive in the Minneapolis-St. Paul area; and John, a professor of English Literature and Writing who also authored texts in his field. Clearly the emphasis on education was a strong priority of both Lloyd and Olive.

When the children were young, the family drove and camped across America exploring the Great Lakes, the Rocky Mountains, the "Patriot Trail" in Boston, and other memorable sites. An accomplished amateur photographer, Lloyd assembled slide shows of these trips and numerous others that he and Olive took throughout the world after their children had grown.

He and Olive also had an abiding fascination with politics. As a result, political discussions were a staple at the Schwiebert dinner table. A Democrat by conversion, Lloyd possessed an abiding belief in the value of good government to improve people's lives. Lloyd also possessed a dry sense of humor, observing on occasion that certain, particularly feckless older politicians provided "living proof that the good die young."

As he grew older, Lloyd's already strong religious faith deepened. A lifelong believer in tithing, he gave generously of his resources as well as his time. At the end of his days, weakened in body but not in spirit, he reflected on a lifetime of successes and setbacks measured by a desire to live a committed life. He could say with some contentment, that like his ideal St. Paul, "I have fought the good fight. I have finished the race—I have kept the faith." (2 Tim 4:7). One valued friend perhaps put it best when she observed "He always took time to care."

Lloyd departed this life on January 22, 2004, mourned and loved by many.

—submitted by his son, Mark W. Schwiebert

Charles Spaulding, Sr.
1928–2005

Charles Edward Alex Spaulding Sr. is the fourth generation to be buried at Chippiannock Cemetery.

Absalom Renfro (1810–1855) married Elizabeth Jane Cormack (1810–1901). Their daughter Mary Ester (1843–1918) married William S. Spaulding (1832–1909). Their son, William A. Spaulding (1868–1941) married Martha Rebecca Thompson (1875–1907). Her parents were James W. Thompson (1840–1903) and Sarah Ann Ewing (1836–1930). William A. and Martha gave birth to William R.B. Spaulding (1900–1977), who married Mabel Scarbough (1900–1948).

Charles Spaulding Sr. was born on February 29, 1928, in East Alton, Illinois, to William R.B. and Mabel. Charles had six brothers—Harold, George, Eugene, Frank, Robert and Harry, and five sisters—Nora Sellers (1920–1964), Virginia Myles (1927–2004), Rose Kelly (1936–1977), Evelyn, and Barb, and a foster sister Helen. He married Dorothy E. Wendt in 1952, and they had five children: Sam, Pat, Judy, Chuck Jr., and Sherri. He also had eight grandchildren and six great-grandchildren.

Life was hard for his family. Many times his parents couldn't care for all 12 children. When that happened some of them would be placed at Bethany Home and into foster homes. Many of these homes were bad and he would run away.

When he was eight years old he was sent to live with the Norris family on a farm. Mr. And Mrs. Norris had two daughters, and a son who had passed away prior to Charles moving in with them. There he was treated like one of the children and was happy, attending country school. He stayed with them until he was old enough to get a job and care for himself, but he stayed close to the Norris family his entire life.

Chuck was employed in the City of Rock Island Street Department for 37½ years. He took great pride in his job. And he loved his two dogs Sissi and Sabrina.

He was outspoken. If he had something to say, he said it, no matter who he was talking to, what the subject was, or where he was. Everyone who met him never forgot him, and would end up with a story to tell about him.

In his younger days he was a great dancer. Many nights he spent at the Rock Island Boat Club with his family, twisting the night away. He enjoyed golfing and would go every Sunday with his brother George. He loved being outdoors. In the summer he was always out in the yard. Sometimes he would sit out side at 3:00 or 4:00 in the morning, waiting for the grass to grow so he could mow it. When the yard work was done he would go fishing.

He was a great dad, although he spent a lot of time working. All of his kids thought of him as Superman, someone who would never die, but they watched him suffer more pain than any person should ever have to suffer. In 2000 he had a stroke which lead to dementia. His health failed him for the next five years, but in August of 2005 it went downhill very quickly. He died on October 4, 2005, at his home in Rock Island. He put up a fight until the very end. He is now in Paradise with his Lord and Savior.

Chuck started a family tradition of giving each grandchild $100 on their 13th birthday. His youngest, Ralph, turned 13 in July of 2005 and fortunately Charles was still alive to bestow this gift.

I miss my dad more than anyone will ever know. I visit his grave almost daily. I know one day we will meet again in Heaven. I miss his mischievous smile most of all.

—submitted by his daughter, Sherri Brown

Richard Swanson
1932–2005

Swanie once described himself as a Jewish, Buddhist, Benedictine, Lutheran Christian. Others called him a bridge-builder, pastor, mensch. The Rev. Richard Swanson was a man ahead of his time, a complex thinker and doer with a simple longing for peace.

Richard Swanson was born on November 22, 1932, in Sycamore, Illinois. While a student at Augustana College, he met Lorian Sundelius, whom he married after graduation in 1954. He went on to earn the Master of Divinity degree four years later at Augustana Theological Seminary and was ordained in the ministry of the Augustana (Lutheran) Synod that same year. After serving a church in Itasca, Illinois, he returned to Rock Island in 1966 as the first pastor of the newly organized Augustana Campus Church, an all-student congregation. And for the next 39 years, he continued his quest for peace.

Swanie searched while he walked, taking daily, often solitary, two-hour constitutionals throughout the Quad Cities. He walked with his family and friends—on Beaver Island in Lake Michigan, through the Grand Canyon, along the Mississippi River. While teaching, he led his students on walks around the campus and to Easter sunrise services on Sylvan Island. After his death, the college dedicated one of his favorite campus walkways as the Swanie Slough Path in his memory.

Swanie was a master with words, but used them sparingly. He discovered that listening brought him much closer to peace than speaking did, agreeing with St. Francis of Assisi, who said, "Proclaim the Gospel at all times, and when necessary, use words."

He listened to his students, colleagues and friends, wife Lorian, his three sons–Scott, Craig, and Kai–and their friends, and eventually their families. When the oppressed began to speak up, he listened, supporting the often-unpopular causes of civil rights, women's rights, gay rights. He read voraciously, listening through the written word to authors and experts and masters.

In his ecumenism he searched, his questions of spirituality creating a disquiet inside him that did not mirror the peace he exuded on the outside. He was an ordained minister of the Evangelical Lutheran Church in America (ELCA), but took his quest far outside the borders of his own religion. Swanie considered himself a Benedictine oblate, a Buddhist, a Quaker. A seeker.

He started a partnership with the Quad Cities Jewish community in the 1970s, helping to create the Quad City Holocaust Remembrance Committee. That organization presented him with its Hope for Humanity Award in 1998, one of only four such awards ever bestowed. Trees were planted in his honor in Israel by the Rauch Family Foundation II and the Jewish Federation of the

Quad Cities a few months after his death in 2005, a living legacy of growth for Jewish community relations that he fostered.

After serving as campus pastor, director of college relations, and dean of campus ministries at Augustana, Swanie retired in 1999. Three years later, the Augustana Sociology Department established the Richard Swanson Professorship of Social Thought.

He had never outgrown being an Eagle Scout and signed up as a volunteer with the Mississippi Regional Blood Center in Davenport, Iowa. He had been a generous donor the past 20 years, donating more than 12 gallons of blood to save the lives of others. As a volunteer, he chose to be a driver, distributing blood any time, anywhere it was needed. Other volunteer works included leading workshops on spirituality for seniors, mentoring newly ordained pastors, and answering telephones and welcoming visitors at St. Mary Monastery.

Swanie died suddenly and unexpectedly on March 10, 2005, of an aortic dissection. Those who knew and loved him hope he has found peace.

—submitted by his wife, Lorian Swanson

Joseph A. Vogele
1912–1993

Joseph A. Vogele was born in Rock Island on February 6, 1912, the son of Ferdinand and Bertha Nachbauer Vogele. He married Helen Carroll (1912–1989) on March 28, 1932, and they went on to have five children: Joseph A. "Tony" Vogele, Jr., Terrence C. Vogele (1935), Jeffrey C. Vogele (1937–2000), Mary H. Vogele Monkus (1943–1976), and Gregory M. Vogele (1950).

Ferdinand ran the Chippiannock Cemetery from 1922 to January 1, 1938, when Joseph took over. In his 38 years of serving as superintendent, Joe never missed leading a funeral to the gravesite. He was always dressed appropriately and reported to the barn promptly each morning to start the employees with their individual assignments. He usually checked with them at 12:30 after lunch, and again at quitting time. During the summer months he would also cruise through the cemetery checking to see that everything was okay and that everyone was working. He had a gift of being able to make the least appealing task into important meaningful work for the person he assigned to complete it. He was adept at breaking down a lawn mower and putting it back together. There wasn't anything he would ask you to do that he hadn't done himself.

Back in those days all graves were dug by hand and he laid out where the grave was to be dug. Not a spade of dirt was turned until he checked out the site. He usually checked to see that the tent was up and everything was in order for the funeral. Back then it was not unusual to have three funerals in one day, so the tent had to be set up, taken down, and set up for another funeral. During his tenure Joe oversaw two large projects—the development of the Centennial section and the paving of the roads in the cemetery.

Decoration Day, now called Memorial Day, was Joe's biggest day of the year. All day long cars were backed up on 12th Street, trying to get into the cemetery so families could visit their deceased loved ones. There was a steady stream in and out of the cemetery starting around 8:00am. Terry, Jeff and Tony used to monitor the cars and run around waving American flags. The following week, it took hours to clear dead flowers and other mementoes off the gravesites.

The family lived in a large house on the cemetery grounds—the house that Joe himself had been raised in. He built a ramp from upstairs in the barn to the fenced-in area for the chickens they raised. The kids remember how tough it was to teach those chickens to run up the ramp from the yard each night. He could identify every species of bird or tree in the cemetery and he loved plants. One room in the house was always filled to overflowing with both common and exotic houseplants.

As soon as they learned to speak, the children called their dad "Joe," because that's what they heard the maintenance crew call him. Joe never corrected them, but in the 1960s, they decided to start calling him Dad and he liked that.

While the children were growing up, Joe was the parent who woke them each morning, fixed their lunches and sent them off to school. In the winter he'd make them a breakfast of hot Cream of Wheat or oatmeal in a double boiler. He taught the kids how to build a fire in the furnace and how to bank the coal in the furnace to keep the house warm over night. One year Tony got an air pistol for his birthday, so Joe set up a target range in the basement. He also showed the three older boys how to shoot a rifle.

Joe could do anything in his children's eyes as they grew up. He built them a camp up on the knoll that had one window in the back, and a picture window and a door that closed in front. They made it comfortable with a couch to lounge on and a wind-up Victrola for music. He was always there when the kids needed help fixing their cars, replacing radiators, rear axles, and you–name–it on the junkers they brought home

Joe was also active in the community. He joined and served in the Illinois Militia, now called the National Guard, stationed at the Armory in downtown Rock Island. The militia protected the citizens at home during World War II in the event of an attack by the enemy. For many years he drove the school bus for St. Mary's School in Rock Island and was active in all the parish events and activities. He was at one time a ranking member of the Lions Club in Rock Island. In later years, Joe and Greg entered the Fourth Degree of the Fr. Bader Assembly of the Knights of Columbus on the same day. He held membership until his death.

To sum it up, Joe was a father and a friend. He may not have created a monument for all mankind in the cemetery, but he raised four sons and a daughter to be good citizens and was proud of the family that he and Helen helped mold.

—submitted by his sons, Tony, Terry, and Greg Vogele

Jack G. Vukov
1949—

I was the first child of Jack and LaVergne Vukov. Born on Sept. 30, 1949, in Berwyn, Illinois, I entered the world "blue" and didn't breathe for a while because my mother had been over-sedated on barbiturates. The doctor feared I would be brain damaged.

In my early years I lived in a duplex with my maternal grandmother. My father would never speak to her; I never knew why.

In 1959 my sister, two brothers and I moved with my parents to Woodridge, Illinois, after my father became co-owner of a business in Downers Grove. My childhood was uneventful—my father was abusive, my mother was moderately supportive.

In adolescence I decided to learn everything I could, contribute, and be someone. Being a medical doctor seemed to be a perfect choice. I graduated from Downers Grove High School South in 1967 and attended Loyola University Stritch School of Medicine after three years at North Central College. I graduated after 3½ years of medical school, *summa cum laude*. I polled older physicians regarding what branch of medicine was the best, and a large percentage said, "be an ophthalmologist."

I was accepted to Loyola's Ophthalmology program without an internship and in November 1976 started my practice in Rock Island. At that time I was probably the youngest board certified ophthalmologist in the country. It's a profession I love to this day.

During my adult years I learned everything possible. I traveled to all 50 states and 60 plus countries. I became an avid white water kayaker, mountaineer, rock climber, windsurfer, scuba diver, bicyclist, snow and water skier, racquetball and tennis player. My motto has been, "Life is one-third work, one-third sleep, and one-third fun."

My "fifteen minutes of fame" came in 1993 when a homeless man broke into my house and lived there for a week. Eventually he ran out of food, found some money, and drove to Andalusia in my Rolls Royce to pick up potato chips. The clerk at the store perceived something was not right and called the police who easily apprehended him. I was bicycling in rural Nova Scotia at the time and nobody could find me. I found out about the incident when I saw my car on a national TV news broadcast while staying in a small Bed and Breakfast.

In 1999 I started the Jack G. Vukov M.D. Foundation Inc. Hopefully it will contribute to society long after I'm gone.

Ever since college I was never at a loss for female companionship but waited until November 1, 2000, to marry at the Kumalani Chapel at the Ritz Carlton Resort in Kapalua, Maui, Hawaii. A choice I never regretted.

I always named my homes. My residence locally was "Timberline" in Illinois City. Many of my summers were spent on my 8-acre "Summerhaven" Island in Lost Bay, Conferation Lake, Ontario, Canada. My mausoleum, to be completed in 2004, is named "Carinya," an Australian aboriginal word meaning *a peaceful and happy place.*

At age 54 I'm in perfect health and I enjoy and make the most of each new day. I fear my life may be cut short. I certainly hope I'm wrong in this regard. My name has never appeared on any Fortune 500 list. Nonetheless, I consider myself to be the richest man in the world.

—submitted by Jack Vukov, M.D.

Families

—Bruce Walters

Ainsworth/Cook Families

Captain Zachariah Cook (1800–1865) and his wife Barbara (1801–1887) moved from Virginia to Rock Island in 1936, accompanied by daughter Mary (1827–1908) and son George (1829–1905). They established themselves as one of the area's original settlers, and the Captain served as one of the County's first treasurers. Daughter Rachel (1841–1848) was born in Rock Island but did not survive her childhood.

In 1853, Mary was wed to Charles Ainsworth (1829–1904), who had settled in Rock Island in 1848 and was owner of Ainsworth & Lynde, a mercantile business on the Rock Island levee. A large part of their trade was forwarding freight by river, but when the railroad came to Rock Island in 1854, business slowed. Seven years after their marriage, Mary and her husband moved to Edgington before settling in Des Moines, where he manufactured plows.

Mary and Charles returned to Rock Island County in 1869, where Charles became associated with Dimock, Gould & Co., manufacturers of washboards, tubs, pails, and lumber. He later served as treasurer and then vice president of the company. In addition, he became a director in the Lindsay Land & Lumber Co. of Davenport, the Musser Sauntry Co. of Stillwater, and was involved in Weyerhaeuser interests locally and in the north.

Mary and her husband entertained many guests in their fine, richly appointed home. On Christmas Day 1903, the couple celebrated their golden wedding anniversary as guests of honor at a dinner party at the Manufacturers' Hotel. Charles died the following year.

Mary was active in the Baptist Church and attended the day before her death in 1908 at age 81. She was survived by her four children, Lucia (Lucy), Calvin, Charles Henry (1858–1929), and Emma, who was married to Stephen Velie, manager of the John Deere Plow Co. in Kansas City.

Charles Henry married Mary Perkins (1863–1943) and they went on to have two children, Charles P. (1901–1991) and Mary Louise (1904–2002).

Charles P. married Sylvia Tower Bullock (1901–1990) and they had four children: Ross Perkins (1923–1924), Virginia (1927), Robert (1928–2003), and Eleanor (1931–1980).

Eleanor attended Moline Public Schools, graduating in January 1949. Her class was the last of the mid-term classes to graduate from Moline High School.

In the fall of 1949, Eleanor entered the State University of Iowa located at Ames, Iowa, where she affiliated with Gamma Phi Beta Sorority. She had decided to study animal husbandry, having become interested in horses at an early age. She wanted to be a rancher's wife, the wife of a western cowboy. Because Eleanor loved the west, she transferred to Colorado Agriculture College, now called Colorado State University, located at Fort Collins, Colorado.

In the summer of 1953 Eleanor married Grant Beck at the Church of the Transfiguration in Moose, Wyoming. The couple had one child, Kathleen Beck, born April 5, 1963, in Jackson, Wyoming.

For about 12 years Grant and Eleanor operated a working ranch near Pinedale, Wyoming, and during those summers also operated a small camp for girls on the ranch. Some summers Eleanor was the counselor for the girls, and some summers she was the head cook. Each girl had her own horse and saddle for the time at camp. The couple was divorced in 1965.

Eleanor held various jobs in Pinedale, Wyoming, and acted as county supervisor for the 1970 census. She continued to operate her ranch until 1975 when she and her daughter moved to Moose, Wyoming.

There, Eleanor worked for the Administrative service of the Grand Teton National Park until she became too ill to continue working. At that point, they moved to Jackson, Wyoming.

Eleanor was a member of the First Baptist Church in Jackson, Wyoming, and was active in the Jackson Fine

Arts Guild. She was also a staunch supporter of the Grand Teton Music Festival.

Eleanor died November 14, 1980, in Jackson, Wyoming.

—submitted by Robert Ainsworth

Aster/Hartz/ Simmon/ Wilson/Colburn Families

John K. Hunter and S. Ann Baker Hunter have a rich heritage associated with Chippiannock Cemetery.

John Hunter's maternal great-grandfather, John Aster (c.1829–1905) was born in Bavaria, Germany; Catherine Iten (1837–1911) was born in Zug, Switzerland; and the couple married in Rock Island, Illinois, in 1856. John operated a bakery, restaurant, ice cream, and oyster saloon on Market Square in Rock Island. He also leased Hillier's Hall, adjacent to the bakery, and rented it out for parties, dances, and suppers. Catherine's father operated the Iten Cracker business in Clinton, Iowa. John and Catherine had a daughter named Emma (1859–1911) and a son named William L, whose son, William R. Aster (1889–1973), was a World War I Army Veteran.

John Hunter's paternal great-grandmother Theresa Boerner Hartz (1833–1888) was born in Altona, Germany. After her husband died, leaving her with eight children, she decided to immigrate to America. Because single women and children were not allowed to make the trip, she remarried, but her new husband died during the journey and was buried at sea. Her children buried at Chippiannock are Ben C. (1856–1932), Adolph (1859–1953), Julius Martin (1863–1955), and Dora (1872–1960). Theresa's daughter Bertha Hartz Buettner married a Presbyterian minister and had a daughter, Edna Buettner Robeson (1890–1969), who is also in the family plot.

Ben C. Hartz was a founder of Hartz and Bahnsen drug company in Rock Island. He married Emma Aster and they had three children: Elizabeth Barton (1884–1954), who was the assistant society editor for the *Daily Times* in Davenport, Ben A. (1892–1972), and Maude (1889–1977).

Maude married J Keith Hunter (1900–1961), the advertising manager of Davenport newspapers. They were the proud parents of Benjamin Hartz Hunter and John K. Hunter (1929–), who was born in Columbus, Ohio. On December 19, 1953, he married S. Ann Baker (1930–) in Rock Island.

Ann Hunter's maternal great-great-grandfather was Phillip Simmon (1818–1897). He was born in Germany and married Catherine Anne Miller (1817–1852) in 1843 in Pennsylvania. One of Rock Island County's pioneers, he was a drayman—a person who drives a long strong cart without fixed sides for carrying heavy loads—and a politician. His second wife, Cornelia Jane Hitchcock (1833–1892) is also at Chippiannock.

Phillip and Catherine's son George (1843–1913) was in the draying business with his father. He married Ingy Robley (1851–1886), who was born in Norway. They were married in Davenport, Iowa, on October 28, 1868, and had two children. Daughter Lillie Viola (1874–1962) married Robert T. Williams (1860–1945). Son Peter Canna (1878–1958) was a mail carrier with the Rock Island Post Office. He married Carrie Eva Colburn (1877–1982) in 1903. Peter died on October 16, three days before his 80th birthday and was buried on October 18, his wife not wanting him to be buried on his birthday.

Both Carrie's maternal and paternal ancestors are buried at Chippiannock. Mark C. Wilson (1804–1876) married Delilah Foor (1808–1897), both of whom were born in Pennsylvania. Their daughter Mary Ann (1840–1920) married Jewett Ziba Colburn (1844–1897), who was born in Vermont. He served in the Civil War and was an engineer for the Rock Island Lines Railroad. His parents were Ziba Colburn (1811–1876) and Mary Perley Craft (1814–1868). Ziba was also born in Vermont and was a carpenter for the Rock Island Lines Railroad.

Mary Ann and Jewett gave birth to Carrie Eva, who married Peter Canna Simmon The couple had two infant sons who are buried on their plot, and one daughter, M. Lorraine Simmon. When Carrie was 100 years old, she traveled to Iowa City to speak at her great-granddaughter's second grade class. She kept their attention for an hour, sharing tales of what her life was like when she was in second grade. She died at age 104.

Peter and Carrie's daughter Lorraine married J. Kenneth Baker, and in Moline, Illinois, they gave birth to S. Ann Baker, who married John K. Hunter.

Thus, between Ann and John, they have seven ancestors at Chippiannock Cemetery who were born 175 to 200 year ago and became pioneers of Rock Island County. Reposing in those family lots are an additional 49 family members.

—submitted by Ann Hunter

Cleaveland and Hayes Families

Henry Clay Cleaveland (1844–1899) was born in Woodstock, Vermont, and attended public schools in Ludlow before entering the machinist trade. At the beginning of the Civil War, he felt the call of duty and was mustered into the First Vermont Volunteers in Company B. After his three-month enlistment expired, he signed up again, this time for a three-year stint as a private in the Sixth Vermont Infantry.

In May, 1862, he was promoted to color sergeant. While serving in the battle at Fredericksburg Heights, he was severely wounded in his arm and both thighs. After recovering, he was commissioned first lieutenant and quartermaster—an army officer who provides clothing and subsistence for troops. Henry was then put in charge of the newly-formed 108th Volunteer Colored Infantry, which was led by white officers. In 1864, his regiment was transferred to the Rock Island Arsenal to serve guard duty for the confederate prisoners of war held there. He was awarded the rank of captain and again served as quartermaster.

After mustering out, Henry chose to make his home in Rock Island, where he wed Olivia Hayes (1848–1909), daughter of William Henry Hayes (1815–1908) and Calista Hatch Hayes (1824–1900). Olivia's sister, Nellie (1859–1944) was married to Arthur Stevens (1861–1891).

As many of Rock Island's settlers became leading industrialists, Henry realized that these growing businesses needed to manage their risk against potential financial loss due to fire or marine catastrophe, and thus made his mark in the city by offering insurance protection. In 1868, he formed a partnership with his father-in-law W. H. Hayes and thus created Hayes & Cleaveland insurance company. Henry organized Mutual Union Fire of Moline, and then Manufacturers Mutual Fire in 1886 and 1888, respectively, but closed them after only a few years of service. He then revived his original company with his son Harry, and it went on to be one of the great western insurance companies.

During his career, Henry served as special agent of the Norwich Union, acted as one of the insurance adjusters for the great Chicago fire of 1871, and was elected to the Illinois Legislature's House of Representatives, where he was an influential member of the insurance committee. In 1874, he and James J. Parks purchased a half interest in the Union Printing Company, which published the *Rock Island Union* newspaper.

In the community, Henry was a grand junior warden of the Illinois Commandery Knights Templar, was a member of numerous other fraternal orders, and served as the Secretary of the Board of Education in Rock Island. Upon his death in 1899, their son Harry Hayes Cleaveland, Sr. continued running the Agency. Henry and Olivia also had a daughter, Bessie, who married William Sweeney, and a son, Louis K. (1872–1933), who was married to Clara (1874–1950) and was employed as assistant chief clerk in the state of Illinois insurance department. The Agency remained in the family until 1982 when Harry Hayes Cleaveland III passed away.

—submitted by Mary Cleaveland, widow of
Henry's great-great-grandson,
Harry Cleaveland III

Dingeldein Family

While many of Rock Island's pioneer settlers established industrial businesses, Philip D. Dingeldein (1822–1897) emigrated from Germany for the purpose of growing grapes and raising cattle in the fertile soil at the confluence of the Mississippi and Rock Rivers.

Philip arrived in 1853 at the age of 31. Within five years he had established a barn, a vineyard, a slaughterhouse, an ice house, a chicken coop, and a home that also served as a wine hall. Since the house stood halfway between Milan and Rock Island, it became known as The Half-Way House (and also Dingeldein Wine Hall), a place where travelers could stop for a refreshing sip of wine.

In 1860 he expanded his ventures, opening a meat store on Second Avenue. Four years later he entered into a partnership with George F. Wagner to run a butchering business. That enterprise thrived as they supplied beef to the railroad and the river boats. And while running the meat business, his 12-acre vegetable garden grew to 50 acres.

Dingeldein had four children, Mary, Maggie, Philip and Henry. Nothing is known about their mother except that she was not involved in rearing the children. Realizing the children needed a mother, Dingeldein contacted Elizabeth (1843–1926), a young woman he had known in Germany, and proposed that she come to the United States to marry him and help raise his children.

Philip Dingeldein began to suffer from spinal trouble in 1894 and died three years later at the age of 75. After his death, his son, known as Philip Sr. (1855–1946), closed the wine hall. Not wanting his daughters to be raised in a tavern, he converted that part of the building into living quarters for his wife Emma Dierolf (1866–1906) and their children Meta (1885-1965), Ella Criswell (1890–1976), Mary (1894–1981), Margaret Applegate (1896–1974), Emma (1898–1996), and Philip Jr. He also removed all but three of the grape vines that his father had brought over from Germany and used that land to plant more vegetables.

Philip Jr. (1892–1967) and his wife Evelyn Mills (1901–1987) worked their whole life at The Dingeldein Gardens with their children John Philip and Elizabeth. James Edward (1932–1933) died as an infant. Philip Jr. left the business only long enough to serve as an Infantryman in World War I. His son, John, still has his father's helmet.

John (1930) was born in Moline, but grew up in the original Rock Island home built by his great-grandfather three generations earlier. John followed in his father's footsteps and enlisted in the Army in 1953. He was stationed in Goose Bay, Labrador, and was part of the contingency that built the air base in Thule, Greenland.

In 1954 he married Rosalyn Michel (1931) and when he was released from the Army in October of that year, took over the family business. Once their children—Philip, Michael, Lisa, and Paul—were all in school, Rosalyn started working in the retail part of the business. Although they continued to raise vegetables, in the 1970s they added a greenhouse and began selling bedding plants as well. They retired in 2001 and set out to explore the USA.

John is interested in politics and golfing. John's son Philip currently lives in the house with his wife, Shelly, and their children—the sixth generation of Dingeldein's to live in the original home, where the trunk Elizabeth brought with her from Germany sits in the attic.

—submitted by
John Philip Dingeldein

Downing Family

George C. Downing (1825–1904) was born in Coalbrookdale, Shropshire, England and was educated there in the common schools. At age 14 he began learning the trade of iron moulder. He and Jane York (1823–1892) were married in 1845, and 12 years later immigrated to Rock Island County, Illinois. George was involved in the foundry business for many years and also owned a farm at New Windsor, Illinois. In 1897, George, at age 72, married Elizabeth York, who had nine children by her first husband.

George and Jane had seven children: Mary Jane, Joseph, George C. Jr., John Edward, Elizabeth G., James, and Thomas. Elizabeth (1857–1864) was born in New York while the family was en route to Illinois. She burned to death when she was just a child.

James (1861–1934) was born in Rock Island and took up the foundry trade. In 1887 he married Rebecca A.

Lawler (1863–1931) and they moved to Bowman, North Dakota to farm. He committed suicide by hanging himself in the basement of the Waterhouse Hotel, where he was living and receiving medical aid. The couple had five children.

John Edward (1855–1924) was born in England and married Laura Kreis in Rock Island. He, too, joined the family in the foundry business and served as a road commissioner. In 1909 he went into the dairy business, which was renamed Downing Brothers Dairy when his sons James, Harry, George, and Ben took it over. The couple also had a daughter, Jennie (1881–1936), who died of tuberculosis, and a son, John Edward Jr. (1886–1916), a teamster by trade who died of pneumonia. Their son George York married Helen M. Johnson whose children were Marilyn and Donald George. Donald married Geraldine A. Dowden, who had twins Donald York and Karen Joyce Downing Rascher.

Mary Jane (1848–1920) was also born in England. In 1870 she married Conrad Schmidt who had emigrated from Germany and changed his name to Smith. The couple had four children: John E., George C., Mary Jane "Mayme," and Louis. George C. married Emily and they had Louis (1897) and Harry C., who married Mildred Adelaide Johnson.

Their children were twins (who died at birth), Harriet Smith Olson, and Franklin Robert. When Mary Jane's husband Conrad died at age 30, she moved to the New Windsor family farm with brother Joseph and his family. Later she moved with her brothers to What Cheer, Iowa. There she met and married Thomas Manuel (1838–1922), a veteran of the Civil War who was born in Wales. He was a coal miner and Assistant Street Commissioner.

Mary Jane and Thomas had three children, Richard York, Laura E., and Louis Thomas. Richard York (1886–1969) married Elsie A. Hanshaw (1888–1939). He started as a machine operator on Arsenal Island, then worked as a painter for area contractors for more than 50 years. They had five children. A year after Elsie died, Richard married Marie Louise DeJonckhaare Mesure (1887–1979). Marie was born in France and had outlived two husbands before marrying Richard.

Thomas married Annie Florence Bostock and had six children, including William Edward (1892–1979). William started working at age 17 as a clerk at a railroad company, became an assistant purchasing agent for a plow shop, then served 16 years as Superintendent of the Centennial Bridge Commission. He was a member and past president of the Rotary Club, was active in Boys Scouts of America for more than 30 years, a member of Rock Island Lodge No. 658 AF & AM, the Royal Arch Masons, Chapter 18, Rock Island Commmandery No. 18, and the Modern Woodmen of America.

In 1914 William married Florence A. Johnson (1890–1964), whose parents were born in Sweden. She was a member of Trinity Episcopal Church, the Vestment Guild of the church, Mary Lowe Dickinson Circle of King's Daughters, Rock Island YWCA, Davenport Outing Club, and served as an aide to the executive director of Bethany Home. The couple had one daughter, Madelyn Florence (1917–1960), who married Donald L. Olson, Sr. (1918–1965). In 1966 William married Evelyn E. Eckhart (1898–1985).

George C. Downing's brother, John (1828–1908), who was also born in England, followed his brother to Illinois 13 years later on the ship Louisiana. He was a pattern maker and a carpenter. In 1849 he married Mary Ann Milner (c.1829–1890), the daughter of an iron moulder in Yorkshire County.  The couple had eight children, all of whom made the voyage with their parents: George S., Charles, Ambrose Henry, Elizabeth Sarah Anne, Martha Ann, Mary Jane Milner, Adelaide Milner, and Randolph.

Randolph (1867–1912) and Charles (1852–1878) never married. Randolph was a carpenter like his father, and Charles was a moulder like his Uncle George. George S. (1850–1904) was a member of the Moline Iron Moulders Union. He married an Iowa girl, Lillie E. Young (1858–1937), whose parents emigrated from Germany. The couple had two children, Blanche (1880–1882) and Estella.

Ambrose Henry (1855–1901) worked as a pattern maker, a moulder, and a day laborer. He was married to Rosa Strupp (c.1857–1899), who died of blood poisoning after suffering an accident. The couple had eight children, Charles A., Roy Randolph, Lotta, Irwin Henry, Elizabeth Rosa, Grace Daisy, Carl W., and Martha A. Lotta (1886–1888) and Grace Daisy (1893–1895) both died of croup as toddlers. Martha and Carl were adopted by the Behrends family of Whiteside County. Charles A. (1882–1927) married Gertrude "Birdy" Parks and they had nine children, including Walter (1917–1922), who died of a ruptured appendix. Charles died at Pine Knoll Sanatorium of tuberculosis.

Martha Ann (1859–1954) was educated in the Rock Island schools along with her siblings. In 1878 she married Charles Phillip Strupp (1854–1897), the brother of Rosa Strupp Downing. They had six children: Daisy Grace, Charles Peter, Violet Marguerite Kinne, Myrtle, Earl Grover, and Margarita (c.1880–c.1884) who died after sustaining burns. Martha Ann was active in the Bethany Home sewing circle, John Buford Women's Relief corps No. 66 auxiliary to the Grand Army of the Republic, auxiliary to the Sons of the Union Veterans of the Civil War, the Woman's Patriotic Association, and the Memorial Christian Church. In 1905, Martha Ann married August Benjamin Beck (1859–1943). As her great-grandson, Earl Louis Strupp III tells it, she had a good business sense, was good with money, and was a good card player. Furthermore, "she was also known to occasionally cheat at cards, but other than that was a very lovable lady."

Martha Ann's son, Earl Grover (1892–1977), had a good head for business, too. He started out as a laborer at an oil company and worked his way up into management. He married Hazel Eckhart (1894–1975), whose father once belonged to the Looney Mob and whose grandfather had been a spy in the Civil War. Hazel served as deputy assessor for South Rock Island Township for 20 years. She was a member of Kings' Daughters Faithful Circle and Central Presbyterian Church, was the first USO worker in the area during World War II, served as president of Irving School PTA, and volunteered over 3,000 hours at East Moline State Hospital. Hazel was the sister of Evelyn Eckhart, who married William Downing, bridge commissioner.

Earl Grover and Hazel's children were Robert, Earl Louis, and Evelyn. Earl Louis (1919) married Julianne Vaughan (1921–1978) and they had five children.

> —submitted by Harriet Smith Olson and Karen Downing Rascher, great-great granddaughters of George C. Downing and Jane York Downing

> —information provided by Downing Family History Association

Ferguson/Bleuer/Lamp Families

Robert Ferguson is related to three families who have lived in Rock Island for over 100 years.

Robert's great-grandparents John Bleuer (1820–1890) and Anna Deiler Bleuer (1826–1901) were born and married in Switzerland. When the couple immigrated to the United States, they brought two children with them and had another child during their two years in New York. After traveling to Rock Island County, Illinois, in 1854, the year the railroad came to that county, they had nine more. A thirteenth child died at birth. John Bleuer Sr. was a carpenter, cabinet-maker, musician, and violin-maker who became a naturalized citizen of the U.S.

Their son Nicholas (1855-1907), a cigar-maker and musician, married Rosina Bladel (1859-1923).

Their son John Jr. (1846-1931) married Christina Scheopf (1850-1943) and they had six children. His wife emigrated from Helmbrecht, Germany in 1851 with her father and her mother, Elizabeth Schoepf (1825-1898). While traveling by steamer from St. Louis, Mr. Schoepf fell overboard just below Rock Island. He drowned with all their money in his pockets. Elizabeth and young Christina were set ashore in Rock Island by the boat officers. There they survived by the kindness of Charles Hengstler, a cigar maker, Adam Schmitt, a furniture storekeeper who ran a boarding house on the levee, and Captain John Peetz. Elizabeth married a second husband, George Durmann, and had two sons, Charles and George C., who was born a few months after his father passed away in 1864. Three years later, she married David Beck, a saloon owner.

John Jr. was an accomplished musician like his father and started Bleuer's Band with his nine brothers. When he turned fifty in 1896, he stated that "they boosted me out," and the band was taken over by his brother Ben, who was 26 years younger than John Jr.

Benjamin Fay Sr. (1872-1946) married Rose Henrietta Neomi Lemburg (1877-1953). He worked for the City of Rock Island in the Street Department, eventually serving two terms as Superintendent of Streets. Besides being a skilled violin maker, he provided the music and stepped up as conductor of the band in 1901. They performed in the city's Empire, Harper, and Illinois

Theaters, as well as the Moline, Illinois, theater and the Burtis Opera House and American Theater in Davenport, Iowa.

Benjamin and Rose had six children. Their sons were Benjamin, Jr., Alfred (1906–1924), and Paul Henry (1908–1964) who married C. Adele Haines-Murray and later married Fay L. Lamb. Paul Henry owned and operated the Peaches and Cream Tavern in downtown Rock Island. Their daughters Ethel Anna (1900–1972), who was employed at Royal Neighbors of America, and Erma Neomi (1910–2000) never married.

Their daughter Helen married Vance Ferguson. The couple had one son, Robert, and a daughter, Helen Marie Norton. Vance's parents were Samuel Jacob Ferguson (c.1864–1913) and Annie Laurie Easter (1869–1952). Vance had a sister Sula M. and a brother Kenneth E.

Samuel graduated from Lebanon Normal School in Lebanon, Ohio and taught for a few years before becoming principal of Reynolds High School. It was during his four years there that he developed his lifelong interest in the rural school system. His success in that district garnered the attention of the rest of the county, and he was elected Rock Island County Superintendent of Schools, an office he served for four terms. Samuel was one of the earliest proponents of adding scientific agriculture to the rural school curriculum and worked to secure 20 college scholarships for boys attending rural schools. He was past president of the Northern Illinois Teachers Association, was a prominent member of the Twin-City Teachers Association and the Tri-City Schoolmasters Club, and past manager of the Illinois State Teachers Reading Circle.

He and Annie were members of the First Methodist Church, where he taught and served as superintendent of the Sunday School, and organized the Men's Brotherhood of the church, serving as its president for a term. In addition, Samuel served as prelate of Rock Island Commandery No. 18 Knights Templar, high priest of Rock Island chapter No. 18, R.A.M, and eminent commander of Rock Island Commandery. He was a member of Rock Island Lodge No. 658 A.F. and A.M. and the Kaaba temple of the Mystic Shrine of Davenport, Iowa.

Annie also received a degree from Lebanon Normal School, graduating at the head of her class, and earned an additional degree from Oberlin College in Ohio. She taught school in Tennessee for one year and in Arkansas for one year before moving to Rock Island. After her husband passed away, Annie got a job teaching English at Rock Island High School and worked there from 1915 until her retirement in 1937. Besides her church involvement, she was a member of the P.E.O. Sisterhood.

Robert's great-great grandparents, Claus Hinrich Lamp (1834–1929) and Antje Ewoldt (1833–1906) were born and married in Germany and immigrated to Rock Island in the spring of 1866. The couple had six daughters and three sons. Claus worked for Bailey Davenport for 24 years, supervising all of the outdoor work on the Davenport estate, which covered most of the south-central portion of Rock Island. After Mr. Davenport's death, Claus continued as caretaker under the employ of the estate's attorney, Col. Henry Curtis, for 22 more years.

In 1928, Claus, then age 93, was interviewed by John Hauberg, spilling the intimate details of Colonel Davenport's illegitimate children and other family secrets. He also remembered when "Chippiannock cemetery had corn hills—old Indian cornfields and the little mounds were pretty high."

The couple's son Edward (1868–1957) was born in Rock Island. He married Anna Marie Schmid (1867–1952) and they had four boys and two girls. Edward was in the plumbing business for nearly 60 years and loved gardening. Both were active members of the Evangelical Church of Peace.

Claus and Antje's daughter Minnie (1860–1934) was born in Germany. She married Henry Lemburg Sr. (1850–1925), who was also born in Germany and became a naturalized citizen in February 1875. He had one brother who was lost at sea. Henry was a co-owner of the Rock Island Brewery and of Mott, Winter & Company, a wholesale liquor dealer. He also served as president of the Rock Island Mutual Building Loan & Savings association for 15 years and was a member of the Odd Fellows of Rock Island. Their daughter Rose Henrietta Neomi married Benjamin Bleuer, whose daughter Helen married Vance Ferguson and gave birth to Robert when Vance was 44 years old.

Robert attended Irving School, where he had the same 6th grade teacher as his father had—Miss Maude Graham. He attended Franklin Jr. High, which has been razed, and remembers when Central High School burned. He loved to watch the crews as they constructed the Centennial Bridge and the television tower in downtown Rock Island.

When Robert was growing up, if he got into trouble somewhere, the news always got home before he did, because everyone knew him. He once fell through the ice on one of the old ponds in Longview Park, and also fell off the animal statue there. He thought he was going to die one day when he was about 11 years old and rode his bike down the 17th Street hill. It was around that time that a boy his age had died going down that road on his bike, through Longview Park, and ran into a light post.

The change in Rock Island that always disturbed Robert was when Spencer Square was converted to the post office. "You never get things like that back." His family lived on 43rd Street until 1944 when his parents moved to California. He now lives in Oregon and his sister resides in Alaska.

—submitted by Robert Ferguson

Franing/Bendt/ Andrews Families

Richard Edward Franing has numerous paternal and maternal relatives buried at Chippiannock Cemetery.

Richard Franing's paternal great-grandfather, C. Louis (Lewis) Franing (1810–1871) was born Christian Ludwig Froehning in the village of Meissen, Westphalia, Germany. He emigrated to the U.S. in 1838 settling in western Pennsylvania. Mary Johanna Martin (1831–1916) was born in Swarzenbach, Bavaria Germany. In 1851 the couple was married in Mercer County, Pennsylvania, and subsequently moved to Rock Island County, Illinois.

There they bought land several miles south of Milan and farmed for a living. Lewis was killed in an unfortunate farm accident on Dec. 10, 1871, taking to his grave the secret that he had actually been born nine years earlier than he claimed, probably fearful that his wife's family would not allow the marriage if they knew the truth, since she was only 19 years old at the time.

The couple had ten children: Emily, Louisa, Elizabeth, Harriet, George, William, John, Edward, C. Lewis, and Henry.

Louisa (1863–1946) and her husband Franklin H. Caldwell (1862–1924) were the parents of Warren, Odessa, Ellmer (1890–1894), Gertrude (1892–1915), and Marjorie (1904–1980). Marjorie was an accountant for several businesses and never married. Her hobby was handwriting analysis. She was a well-known pioneer in the field, authoring several manuals and training hundreds of people. She was the organist for St. Paul Lutheran Church in Davenport, Iowa, for many years.

Emily (1854–1909), Elizabeth (1865–1959), Hattie (1871–1953) and C. Lewis (1867–1907) were never married and are buried in their parents' lot.

C. Lewis Franing became a lawyer and resided in Chicago. His monument in Chippiannock is in the form of a book standing open on the front edge. It reads: "Known to this community all his life. 15 years a lawyer in Chicago. Author of several manuals on law. A conscientious scholarly Christian man who loved his neighbors as himself."

Richard's grandfather, Henry Lewis Franing (1852–1932), was the town druggist in Milan for over 50 years. He was hit by a model T Ford and killed crossing the main street of Milan at the age of 80. He was married to Anna Elizabeth Caldwell (1862–1925). They had two children: Carlise (1893–1895) known as a "blue baby" and Russell Lowell Lawson (1899–1984).

Richard's father, Russell Lowell Lawson Franing, married Lillian "Lillie" Claudina Bendt (1897–1954) and they had two children, Darlene Harriett Hammond and Richard Edward. Russell enlisted in Army and served in World War I. He was a 1923 graduate of Augustana College, then taught Chemistry and Physics at Elgin Academy and Dundee High School (Illinois) and coached football. He earned a Masters Degree at the University of Iowa and entered the University of Chicago Medical School in 1928, completing one and a half years when the  Depression hit, forcing him to drop out of medical school.

The couple returned to Milan, where Russell worked for State of Illinois before becoming employed in 1937 by International Harvester in East Moline as a Material Handling Engineer. After Lillie's death, Russell married Hazel Thomas in 1955, and he retired in 1962.

Richard Edward Franing, a 1963 graduate of Augustana College, married Judith Anderson, an elementary school teacher, in 1971. He worked on the Rock Island Arsenal as an engineering technician until his retirement in 1999. Their two children are Sara Renee and David Richard.

Richard Franing's maternal grandfather, Otto Bendt (1877–1927), was born in the village of Haseldorf, Holstein, Germany, the eldest son of Henry Bendt and

Margaret Bartels. His family emigrated to the U. S. in 1881 and settled in Rock Island where his parents were produce farmers. Otto married Hulda Behrens (1878–1923) and became a produce farmer himself in Rock Island. They had three children: Otto Fred (1901–1972), Mildred (1904–1979), and Lillian Claudina Bendt Franing (Richard's mother.)

Otto's brother, Emil H Bendt (1879–1971) married Helena Pewe (1880–1957) and had nine children: Helen, Pearl, George, Viola, Henry, Eleanor, Bonnie, Alice, and Emil (1908–1924).

Otto's Aunt Metta Bendt (1851–1908) married Heinrich Johannes Christian Andrews (1863–1929) in Germany and traveled to Rock Island for their honeymoon. Mr. Andrews was a millwright by trade and was employed for 27 years at Weyerhaeuser & Denkmann mills. The couple had three infants who died, all named Christian (1889), (1890), and (1891). Also buried in the Andrews family lot are Metta's brother, Michael Bendt (1846–1903), and Christian's niece, Mathilda (1904–1906), who died while visiting from Germany.

Metta and Christian's four surviving children were Henry, Amanda, Minnie Rose, and Edward Christian. Amanda (1887–1970) married Frederick "Oscar" Stapp (1880–1963) and had two daughters, Martha and Eleanor. Edward (1908–1968) married Marion Virginia Mathews and they had one son.

Minnie Rose (1884–1971) married Ludwig Stapp, Sr. (1873–1930). Ludwig was the son of John Stapp (1838–1924) and Katherine Peetz (1846–1931). Minnie had a floral design shop for 22 years, working closely with Ludwig in the L. Stapp greenhouses and floral firm. They had three children, John, Ludwig, Jr., and Marjorie.

John (1905–1933), who never married, committed suicide by driving his vehicle into a concrete bridge railing on Route 67. He served as President of the L. Stapp company floral firm originally established by his grandfather, John Stapp. It was one of the largest in the midwest, engaging mostly in wholesale business. Ludwig, Jr., known as Bud, (1906–1941) also never married.

Marjorie Isabelle (1910–1984) married Robert Bruce Collins, MD (1908–1979). Their children are Clive Collins (1935–1947), Marcia Day Collins Ross, and Ellen Stapp Collins Bahnsen.

—submitted by Richard Edward Franing

Gitt/Ailes/Berg/ Skarp Families

Nannie Ailes (1865-1929) was the daughter of Isaac Ailes (??–1903) and Elizabeth Burrows (??–1897). Isaac was married three times and fathered a total of 21 children, including George (1859–1922), who married Ida (1872–1928); Sadie (1867–1902) who married Julius Crist (1863–1926); Nettie (1875–1956); Robert (1880-1908), who drowned in the Rock River while running the Chutes at Watchtower Amusement Park where Black Hawk Park now sits; Susie (1883–1961), who married Julius Crist, widower of her sister Sadie; and Grover (1884–1944).

George and Ida's children were Olive (1891–1982) and her husband John Danielson (1885–1956); Maebell (1985–1959); and John (1896–1949).

Sadie and Julius' children were George (1892–1948) and his wife Mae (1897–1967); Jamie (1893–1962) and his wife Mae Scott (1889–1961); Elsie (1897–1982); Grace (1902–1979); and DeWitt.

Susie and Julius' children were: Lora (1907–1939) and Etha (1917–1990).

Nannie was a practical nurse who accompanied doctors on many baby deliveries. She was well known as a performer in plays and public readings. She was a member of the Eastern Stars and once served as Worthy Matron, Royal Neighbors of America, Oakleaf Camp #1495, and the Presbyterian Church. She started a family tradition by keeping scrapbooks of songs, poems, articles and pictures of family, friends, local and other interests.

Nannie married Jacob W. Gitt (1857–1925) in 1881. He was a painter and paper-hanger by trade, and was a member of Modern Woodmen of America. Their children were DeWitt (1883–1964), Ida Mae Hardin (1884–1956), Maydie Elizabeth Berg (1893–1945), a son and a daughter who died at birth.

Their daughter Maydie gave piano lessons as a young woman and often visited her sister Ida's family in Preemption, Illinois. There she met their hired man, Gustaf J. Berg (1886–1959), who emigrated from Sweden when he was 16 years old. After attending school, he was a fireman on excursion boats that traveled the Mississippi River between Rock Island and New Orleans.

Later, he worked on the Wilmerton family farm and nearly escaped death. One night Mrs. Wilmerton asked him to walk to nearby Preemption to mail a letter. When he was halfway across the field, the house blew up, completely demolishing the structure. Miraculously, everyone inside escaped without serious injury. The notorious gangster John Looney was suspected, as he considered Mr. Wilmerton to be one of his enemies, but the cause turned out to be a faulty furnace. After the house was rebuilt, George and Ida Gitt Hardin moved in and took over the farm.

Maydie and Gust were married in 1911 and soon after began operating a dairy farm. They had three children who died at birth—Harry, Dorothy, and Robert—and then three healthy daughters, Eda Lucile (1919–), Linnea Grace (1921–) and Betty Lou (1934–). Their home was always a gathering place for their neighbors, friends, and relatives. During the Great Depression, many people could not afford milk,  even though it cost only three cents a quart. Maydie and Gust often gave food to those less fortunate, sending fresh produce home with their visiting relatives to give to needy neighbors.

Gustaf was one of Rusty Campbell's first flying students at the Franing Field in Moline, now Quad Cities International Airport. He flew every Sunday and considered buying his own plane to fly the mail, but his biggest thrill was seeing his hero Charles Lindbergh, who once made a stop at Franing Field.

Gustaf's brother, Carl Knute Berg (1904–1973) emigrated from Sweden in 1923 to live with his brother's family, helping them on the dairy farm before purchasing his own lot and building his bachelor home across the road. He enjoyed collecting antiques and clocks, and attending the Indianapolis Races and the

Kentucky Derby. He was a veteran of World War II and was a charter member of the Reynolds American Legion Post. Carl worked for J.I. Case Company in Rock Island as a carpenter, retiring in 1965.

Maydie and Gustaf's daughter Eda Lucile started school in Preemption, then attended Milan schools when her parents bought the Shady Brook Dairy Farm in that town. In 1940, while working as a nanny for a relative's son in Chicago, she attended the WLS Radio Barn Dance broadcast every Saturday night. A year later she moved back to Milan, riding with Arkie "The Woodchopper" Ossenbrink, WLS radio personality, and his wife Vera. He sold her one of his custom-made Martin guitars, complete with his name inlaid with mother of pearl. In the 1960s, Eda donated that guitar to the Country Hall of Fame Museum in Nashville, Tennessee. For the presentation, she was accompanied by a busload and five carloads of members of the Mississippi Valley Country and Western Music Association of Western Illinois and Eastern Iowa, a group she founded.

In 1941, Eda became employed in the Accounting Department of Bituminous Casualty Corporation in Rock Island and worked there until her retirement in

1984. In the early 40s, she and her sister Linnea played and sang at local events and on WHBF Radio as the "Berg Sisters" and the "Neighbor Girls" on an early morning program called "The Waker Uppers."

Eda became a member of the Milan First Presbyterian Church and the Moline Women of the Moose Lodge, where she served as Mooseheart Chairman. Throughout her life, she was involved with Camp Fire Girls, Queen Esther Circle, Nobel Lodge #288, Vasa Order of America, and the Rock Island County Historical Society. At the request of the Rural Youth group, she organized and led the Milan 4-H Club for many years. Her current hobbies include music, scrapbooks, photography, and collecting cookbooks, dolls, coffee mugs and other items.

Maydie and Gustaf's daughter Linnea attended Milan School and Rock Island High School. In 1937, was offered a job as relief operator at the Milan Telephone Office because she had such a good speaking voice. The following year, she married Viking Skarp (1909-1999), a Swedish immigrant who worked for her father at the dairy, and as a painter and paper-hanger for her Uncle DeWitt. He was very talented in his trade and a genius at mixing and matching colors and patterns. After the death of DeWitt, he worked for Pearson's Decorating in Moline, retiring in 1974.

Viking was well-known to family and friends as an excellent gourmet cook and was a kind, quiet, giving man, always willing to lend a helping hand. He was a member of First Presbyterian Church, Swedish Olive

Lodge, Viking's Club, Independent Order of Odd Fellows for more than 60 years, and a lifetime member of International Brotherhood of Painters and Allied Trades Local 502.

After their marriage, Linnea continued to work at the telephone company, which started as one switchboard, but grew to five boards in World War II. After her supervisor's death and the enlistment of another operator, she became the youngest Agency Manager of the Illinois Bell Telephone Company at age 19.

Although the couple was never blessed with children of their own, they played an influential part of many youngsters' lives. When Linnea's mother died in 1945, she left her job to help raise her younger sister, Betty Lou, who was only eleven years old. She was a Sunday School teacher for 16 years at First Presbyterian Church in Milan, and directed the junior choir at one time. The couple served as Godparents to two nieces, Susan Kay Tobin Schneider and Linda Rae Tobin, and to Lynette Christensen Mohrmann, daughter of friends, and they loved and cared for many more children of family and friends.

In 1957, Linnea became employed at the Moline Public Hospital as the telephone operator supervisor and remained there for 26 years, experiencing progress in technology from the old plug-in cords to modern computerized systems.

Throughout her life, she was involved with Camp Fire Girls, Queen Esther Circle, Rural Youth, and her sister Eda's 4-H club. She was a member of the Friendly Workers in her church, a bridge club, Pythian Sisters,

Milan's Loyal Order of Kings Daughters, Rock Island County Historical Society, and was the first president of the Moline Public Hospital's Retirees' Club. She took care of Viking for several years after he suffered a stroke and heart attack.

Inspired by her grandmother Nannie and her mother Maybie, Linnea creates scrapbooks and photo albums. These have been used as reference by many people, including those who compiled the Milan Book, *Travels in Time*.

—submitted by Linnea Berg Skarp

Herrmann Family

Andreas Herrmann (1830–1915) was born in Wildhaus, Switzerland, a mountain village in the Alps. In 1854, he married Regula Rissi (1833–1907) in the Reformed Church at Azmoos. She was born in Oberschan, St. Gallen, Switzerland, the daughter of Christian Rissi and Regula Leuzinger. Andreas and Regula had eight children in Switzerland, three of whom died in infancy. Those living were Regula, Andrew Hermann (1858–1949), Christian, Barbara, and Heinrich (Henry).

Around 1865, Regula Herrmann's mother and twin brothers, Ulrich and Heinrich Rissi, immigrated to Rock Island, Illinois. Five years later, Regula and her five children came to visit and decided to stay. Andreas was not happy when she wrote to him telling him to join her, as she refused to return to Switzerland. A family story says that the family was so poor in Switzerland that Regula would take as much cow manure from the neighbors as she could, since a pile of cow manure in front of your house meant that you were well off.

Andreas did join his family in America, but refused to learn English. He had been a carpenter in Trubbach and had built chalets there. In Rock Island, he built most of the houses on 13th Avenue between 25th and 30th Streets.

In Rock Island, the couple had two more children, John and William. As an infant, William became deaf when a firecracker exploded near his ear. He and John were not as close to the rest of family, probably because they spoke "American", while the others held onto their old country ways and their Schwietzer-Deutsch language.

Most of their children, upon getting married, moved into houses on the same street next door or across from each other. They also married neighbors and people living nearby. Barbara wed neighbor George Long and her brother Christian married George's sister Agnes, making their children "double cousins."

When Andreas was around 80 years old, he and his son Henry built a boat at the Kahlke boatyards, christening it *Grandpa*.

The plot containing Andreas, Regula, and Andrew had no gravestone, so in 1996, their descendants planted a larch tree as a memorial. Larch trees grow in the Alps and are the only evergreen tree to shed needles in the winter when other trees lose their leaves. The cemetery then installed a granite memorial next to the tree and inscribed it with their names and birth and death dates.

Andreas and Regula's son John Herrmann married and had a son Harry, who married Catherine Asay. Her mother was Myrtle Kaskadden, whose father was John McKinney Kaskadden. His parents were Robert Clarence Kiskadden (later known as Kaskadden) (1823–1885) and Margaret Jane McKinney (1830–1891). According to the Rock Island County Biographies, Robert was 5'8" tall, had dark eyes, auburn hair and a dark complexion.

Robert was a blacksmith in Rapids City, Illinois. At age 41, he left his wife and 10 children to enlist in the 47th Illinois Infantry, Company G. He was discharged a year later as a private in Selma, Alabama, on January 21, 1866. After the war, he and Margaret had three more children.

Harry and Catherine Hermann had a son, Gerald Herman (1927), who married Shirley A. Lowman (1929). Shirley is the daughter of Nevin Lowman (1904–1988) and Doris Edris (1909–1991), who were both born in Indiana and married in Huntington, Indiana, in 1938. As young people they were caught in the throes of the Great Depression, which affected the lives of many.

Soon after their marriage, Nevin and Doris moved to Rock Island, traveling there on the Rock Island Rocket, because Nevin had just taken a job as assistant manager of the Fort Armstrong Hotel. They quickly made Rock Island their home, made many friends, and became members of the First Methodist Church.

When World War II began, Nevin served as a neighborhood Air Raid Warden and Doris worked as a Grey Lady at the T.B. Sanitarium and helped roll bandages for the war effort. After retirement they lived on a lake in Arkansas for a few years, but returned to Rock Island to be near their daughter, Shirley, and to live out the remaining years of their lives among family and friends.

—submitted by Shirley Herman

Schneider/Wieland/Foley Families

Andrew Schneider (1827–1881) and his wife Christine Schneider (1832–1867) operated a boarding house, called Cape Horn House, which served as a small hotel on the banks of the Mississippi River in downtown Rock Island, Illinois. They had four children, including Christine (1857-1940) and Catherine, who loved to watch the many boats and the pilots and captains who operated them. Some people disembarked for a short visit, others to settle in the pioneer town, and still others were going on to a different town inland. They all praised the pilots who got them safely through the rapids and from town to town.

    Of all the captains and pilots, Capt. Daniel Smith Harris of the Steamer Grey Eagle was considered the very best. On May 9, 1861, he was at the wheel of the 250-foot, 382-ton sidewheeler when it smashed against the piling of the much-hated Rock Island bridge. She sunk up to her pilot house almost instantly, sending her crew, 58 passengers, and the freight of grain and flour into the raging river.

    Many people, including Andrew, jumped into their john boats and skiffs to help get the passengers and crew to shore. Thousands more watched from the banks of the river in Rock Island and Davenport. Most of the cargo was lost, and seven people died, including a passenger who had been labeled "insane" on the

manifest and thus had been chained to the deck. After everyone was accounted for, Capt. Smith tried to salvage what he could from the wreck. Andrew was given one of these salvaged items, a pitcher, for his part in helping bring the salvaged materials to a warehouse.

Andrew's daughter Christine got married to George F. Wieland (1851–1897) and had seven children: Henry (1879–1953), George (1881–1943), William (1884–1889), Clara Wieland Foley (1886–1960), Emma Wieland Winkler (1890–1955), Gertrude Wieland Lerch (1895–1924), and Andrew.

Andrew's other daughter, Catherine, married Jensen, a railroad man, and moved to Chicago, taking the pitcher with her. Catherine had five children, none of whom married, including her daughter Kathryn.

Christine continued to live in Rock Island, raising her children and running the boarding house, which had been renamed the Hotel Boarding House and Saloon, then later the Franklin House, and finally the First Avenue Hotel. Her daughter Clara married William Foley and they moved to Blue Island, Illinois, where William worked in the steel mill. Their children were Kathlyn Foley (1914–1972), Kenneth Foley (1921–1936), Mary Foley DeVries (1912–2006), and William L. Foley.

After World War I, the mill closed. William heard they were hiring steel rollers in Kansas City, so Clara and the children moved in with her mother while her husband went on ahead to Kansas City to secure employment and housing for his family. He died there, so the family remained in Rock Island. Clara got a job in a laundry while the children attended school, carried a paper route, and helped around the house.

Their Grandma Christine had a washing machine that had a handle she had to move back and forth to operate it. She promised Bill that if he helped her with the washing, she would take him for a ride on the ferry boat, which was a real thrill. While working, she would tell Bill all about growing up by the river and seeing all the boats, eulogizing the pilots for their skills in safely maneuvering the treacherous rapids.

Two of Clara's brothers worked for the Corps of Engineers. Andy was the cook and his wife Ada was the baker on Corps of Engineer Quarter Boat 347, which housed and fed the crew of the Dipper Dredge St. Paul. The Quarter Boat had a kitchen and dining room with two long tables that could each seat fifteen, a bedroom for the cooks, a bedroom for the Dredge Master and the Bunk Room, which had double bunks for 20 men when the crew was full.

There was a launch that would take the men back and forth from dredge to quarter boat. Sometimes the rock formations would be so large they had to dynamite them so they could be moved. This was the job that Henry performed.

Andy secured a dishwashing job for their nephew William (Bill) on the quarter boat. When they finished building wing dams in an area, the Corps of Engineer towboat Steamer LeClaire would come and tow the dredge and quarter boat to a new location to build the next wing dams. Once Bill saw the wheel house of that towboat, he had his fill of dishwashing and as soon as he was able, he got a job on a towboat.

At age 21, Bill obtained his First Class Pilots License form Minneapolis to St. Louis, He went on to gain a total of 3600 miles of river, including the Ohio River, Illinois River, the Lower Mississippi River and the Intercoastal Canal. He spent the next 64 years piloting towboats. In the final 10 years, he also piloted the Mississippi Queen and the Delta Queen.

In 1980, Bill and his wife Violet were in Chicago and decided to look up his Aunt Catherine's family, who had owned a florist shop. The only family member still alive was Kathryn. During this visit, Bill mentioned the Steamer Grey Eagle pitcher because his grandmother had always talked about how beautiful it was. His cousin Kathryn still had the pitcher in her china cabinet, and she told him that all the years she and her siblings were growing up, they were never allowed to touch it, just look at it. It was in mint condition.

In 1986, Kathryn decided to enter a nursing home, and she gave the beloved family heirloom to her cousin Bill.

—submitted by Violet Foley

Tanner/Means/Bowen/Dickinson Family

David Bowen was a partner in a shipping firm in Providence, Rhode Island. He and his wife, Elizabeth Folger Chase Bowen, had six children and expected the three boys to follow in the family business. The Folger and Chase families had been mariners for generations. Capt. Mayhew Folger is credited with the discovery of the lost mutineers of the ship *Bounty* on Pitcairn's Island and Timothy Folger is credited with mapping the Gulf Stream of the Atlantic Ocean.

The Folger family had come to America from England in 1636 and had settled mostly on Nantucket Island. The Bowen family originated in Wales and also came to America in the early 1600s. The Bowen family can trace their history back to King Charlemagne through the female lineage. If one is familiar with the exploits of Charlemagne, then adventure, courage, and leadership have long been a family trait.

David Bowen Jr. (1812–1892) went to sea at the age of 12 and sailed to various foreign ports for eight years. He then worked on a steamboat on the Ohio River and eventually into the Mississippi, working on steamboats for 21 years. He settled in Keithsburg, Illinois, with his wife, Nancy Cameron, who died there. They were the parents of Eliza, George Cole (1840–1873), Charles Ross (1842–1875), Sarah Ann (1844–1877), and William.

In 1849 David married Mrs. Mary Stephens Beriman (1818–1882), who took care of his three living children and bore six of her own: Albert Wallace (1851–1928), John Gilbert (1853 stillborn), Elizabeth Jane Snyder (1854–1915), Mary Ellen Annable, Ida Maybelle DeCoudres (1860–1914), and Mina Galt (1862–1900).

About six years later, they moved to Rock Island County, where David went into partnership with Henry Houseman to conduct a large general store. The store went bankrupt during the financial panic of 1857.

In 1859 David climbed Pike's Peak in Colorado, then joined Mr. Houseman in Denver and worked for him until 1867, when he returned to Rock Island. There, David started up his own general store, where his daughters worked with him. He started the first free delivery business from this store. He had an adventurous spirit and loved the outdoors. He also loved music and enjoyed family and friends. He was close to his brother, who had also moved from Providence to Rock Island. He and Gilbert were said to look so much alike that they were often mistaken for twins.

Gilbert Chase Bowen (1819–1896) did not go to sea as his forebears had, but chose to go his own way. He moved to Rock Island in 1855 and married Henrietta "Mary" Moss (1833–1903) the following year. They had ten children: Esther Tanner (1856–1934), David (1858 stillborn), Florence Graves (1860-1930), Gilbert Chase Jr. (1862 stillborn), Gilbert Chase Jr., Frank Lincoln, Amos (1869–1897), Annie Mae McPherrin, Alfred Williams, and Grace Parrish.

The couple ran a grocery store located on 2nd Avenue and 10th Street, at one time owning the whole block of land from 9th to 10th Street. Gilbert was also a tailor and he sewed and laid carpets for the Mitchell & Parsons store in Rock Island. Mary ran the store while Gilbert served in the Civil War.

Gilbert had what he referred to as a spy glass from one of the ships which his family owned. This spy glass was set on top of a cupboard in the home on 2nd Avenue and was later inherited by Gilbert Chase Bowen Jr. He and his family were active members of the Memorial Christian Church in Rock Island.

Gilbert's son, Frank Lincoln, became a minister of the Christian Church and moved to Missouri where he helped establish churches throughout the state. Gilbert's son, Gilbert Jr., owned and operated at least two stores in Missouri and was making a delivery to a mountain settlement when he was drowned.

Gilbert and Mary's daughter, Esther married Alfred Williams Tanner (1855–1912) in 1875. She was a devoted wife and mother to their ten children: Gertrude Mary (1876–1942), Florence Schill (1877–1963), Henrietta Wangelin (1879–1964), Elkanah, Esther Means (1882–1955), Ralph Herman (1885), Cora Alice Dunn, Amos (1888–1960), Bernice (1890–1918), and Hollis Robb.

She was active in her church and she welcomed visitors to her home. Their son Amos helped construct the 15th Avenue Christian Church in Rock Island and also built his home on 31st Avenue. Daughter Henrietta married John Nelson Wangelin in 1902 in a ceremony officiated by Esther's uncle, Rev. Frank Lincoln Bowen.

Esther was very proud of her Folger family lineage which was related to Benjamin Franklin. She told her children stories about the Folger family that had been passed down over the generations and this sparked a great interest in her oldest daughter, Gertrude Mary (1876–1942), who was devoted to her family and work.

Gertrude never married and lived at home to take care of her mother following the death of her father. She wrote letters, traveled, researched, and recorded her family history. It was through this passion that she discovered her mother was the 6th generation from Benjamin Franklin, whose uncle was her mother's great-great-great-great-grandfather John Folger.

Esther taught her second daughter, Florence, how to sew and make dress patterns. Florence went on to become a gifted seamstress and made clothing for many of the influential families in the Rock Island and Moline area such as the Deere/Butterworth; the Deere/Velie; the Denkmann; and the Huesing families.

Esther's fourth daughter and namesake, Esther (1882–1955) married Orlin Hascall Means (1883–1942) in 1908. Their children were Virginia Esther (1909 stillborn); Marion Esther Dickinson (1910–1969); Ralph Vernon; Lawrence Bowen; and Orlin Hascall Jr. (1917–1929).

Ollie, as he was lovingly called by his family was a happy child. He loved to ride his bicycle and play with his two older brothers. He was the apple of his mother's eye. He died at age 12 of congenital heart failure and was greatly missed by all but especially his mother who wrote the poem, *Little Boy of Mine*, which expressed her sorrow and loneliness over his loss. She was a gifted poet who had several of her poems published. She came by her love of writing very naturally as it had been passed down through the Folger lineage from the grandfather of Benjamin Franklin, Peter Folger, who had been a great poet himself.

Marion Esther was the last to carry the name of Esther, the fourth generation to do so. She worked as a secretary for Modern Woodman Insurance Company before her marriage to Frank Albert Dickinson (1909-1974) in

1930. Their children were Larry Means, Darlene, Carol Ann, Donna Lee, and Sharon Kay.

She raised tropical fish and won many awards for them. She was a wonderful cook and liked to crochet when she was younger. Marion enjoyed playing Solitaire and telling her granddaughter stories about her aunts, uncles, brothers, and cousins. She was very proud of her family tree and was also proud of her mother's poetry. She shared these things with her oldest grand-daughter, Mary Ellen, who also pursued genealogy, cooking, and writing.

—submitted by Mary Ellen Eberts

Weckel/Bollinger/Erickson/ Jackson Families

Adolph Weckel (1822–1900) was born in Baden, Germany, and moved to Illinois in 1841. His brother Adam paid for the ocean voyage, so Adolph arrived in America without money but with a willingness to work hard. In 1847, he married Catharine Hiensel (1826–1897). Her parents and five sisters emigrated from Bavaria, Germany, because they had been told that the soil in Illinois City, Illinois, made fine Bavarian china. That proved to be false, so they became farmers instead.

The couple had eight children, but two sets of twin boys died in early childhood. The family lived in the brick home that Adolph and Joseph Taylor had built in 1844 in Rock Island, across the street from the original courthouse. Adolph was involved in community affairs, serving for many years on the school board and as the commissioner of highways.

Through the course of the next 10 years, they steadily bought farm land south of Moline (now 7th to 4th Streets and 28th Avenue to 32nd Avenue), where they eventually moved. The couple farmed 225 acres while raising John—the first child of German heritage born in the county, Louis, Rosa, and Eva Cecelia. Bringing his grain to the Milan mill, Adolph passed through Black Hawk's

village, where he made friends with the Indians and gave them gifts of fruit.

Their youngest child, Eva (1869–1927), was 14 years younger than her next oldest sibling, Rosa. In 1892 she married John Bolllinger (1866–1900) and a year later they had a daughter, Mabel Rose. John didn't want to farm, so they moved to Rock Island, where he got a job at the Arsenal. One hot day, while working on the grounds, he became overheated and drank ice water. He suffered a heat stroke which paralyzed him. He spent 18 months in a sanitarium in Maquoketa, where he regained some use of his arms and legs and was able to return home.

During this time, Eva's parents became old and infirm, so they divided their property among the children and moved in with Eva, where they resided until they passed away, her mother in 1897, her father and her husband in 1900.

In repayment for her kindness and hard work, Eva inherited five extra acres containing the house and barn and other outbuildings, which she rented out. After repairs and taxes, though, there was no profit. To earn money to raise her daughter, Eva took in boarders until her own poor health caused her to rent out part of her house to college and seminary students.

She loved to entertain friends and relatives at dinner parties, and the coffee pot was always on for friends who dropped in. She died at age 58 of heart valve problems. Letters written at the time of her death spoke of her pleasant attitude, her unselfishness and big heartedness, her gentle and sincere nature.

Luckily, Eva did live long enough to see her daughter, Mabel (1893–1978) marry Emil Paul Erickson (1891–1950) and give birth to daughter Lois Allene (1927).

While growing up, Mabel attended Longfellow Grade School. Because times were hard, she had only two sets of clothes, one for play and another for school and church. After graduating from 8th grade, she attended business college at Augustana College and graduated from there in 1909. In honor of the event, her mother presented her with a beautiful gold, closed-faced watch engraved with her initials and the year. She was then hired as a secretary in Charles Hodgson' Insurance office in Rock Island, where she worked until her marriage in 1919. Eight years later, Lois was born, the same year as Eva's death.

Mabel inherited those five acres of the Weckel farm, including the house and the barn , along with some land from 4th to 5th Streets and 32nd Avenue to 33rd Avenue, which Uncle John Weckel named the "Mabel Erickson Subdivision" as it is still called today. Other land was sold to a developer and to the Farmall Gun Club.

Mabel spent her life helping friends and family by driving them to visit relatives in the hospital, shopping for groceries, and going to church. She maintained relationships with her mother's friends and would often take them on a picnic or have them to her home. She also loved to take neighbors and her daughter's friends to picnics and parades, bringing enough provisions for everyone. She never forgot anyone's birthday or anniversary. Her favorite hobby was china painting, and she painted a set of Bavarian china in service for 12, along with many serving pieces, which her daughter still owns.

Mabel's husband Emil was born in Missouri, his parents having emigrated from Sweden in 1877. He graduated from Bonne Terre High School, where he played on the basketball team. At one time he worked as a "sandhog," building the subways in Chicago. He also worked at Williams & White and for John Deere Plow Works, both in Moline.

Emil loved hunting and fishing, loading his own shells and weaving his own fishing nets. He grew a huge vegetable garden every year and liked to play cards. Emil, who had a wonderful sense of humor and was always willing to help his friends and neighbors in times of need, served as a Civil Defense Warden during World War II. He died at age 58 of massive cardiac arrest.

Daughter Lois was born March 20, 1927, at the home of her grandmother, Eva Weckel Bollinger, where Mabel and Emil lived. She attended the same grade school as her mother and Central Junior High School. In 1944, she graduated from Rock Island High School where she played in the band. That December she graduated from Rock Island Business College and was hired at Farmall Works of International Harvester Company, where over the years she served as a typist in the Cost department, then a cost clerk and sometimes the substitute secretary. She also helped out in the former Boot Hobby Shop in Rock Island. Lois attended night school at Augustana College, playing French Horn in its symphony orchestra for two years.

She married Thomas M. Jackson (1919–1999), in 1946 at St. John's Lutheran Church, Rock Island. Thomas, an only child, was born in 1919 in Matherville, Illinois. He was in the Army during World War II and served on Guam, where he was run over by a 2 ½ ton truck, then returned to Rock Island to work as a precision tool grinder at International Harvester Co. Farmall Works.

Tom played guitar and string bass professionally in the Bill Kramer Dance Band in the early 1950s and played in numerous small entertainment bands for years after that. He enjoyed amateur radio and model railroads, sang in the church choir more than 40 years, and received the Lamb Award, given by the Evangelical Lutheran Church of America in recognition of service in the Boys Scouts of America. He was in the Boy Scouts organization for over 60 years, being awarded the Scoutmaster's Key and the Silver Beaver Award. He was also appointed by Mayor Mark Schwiebert to serve on the planning committee of The Keystone Neighborhood in 1995.

In 1951, Tom and Lois became the proud parents of that year's Quad Cities New Year's Baby, Robert William. Almost four years later, they had a second son, Murrell Ross. Lois served as a den mother while her two sons were in Cub Scouts.

She is a life-member of St. John's Lutheran Church, were she served as the coordinator of the Ageless Group for four years. In early years she taught Sunday school, sang in the choir and helped the junior choir. Other organizations she belonged to were the Blackhawk Genealogical Society, Quad Cities Computer Society, Keystone and Columbia Park Neighborhoods, Community Caring Conference, and Coalition of Rock Island Homeowners.

She enjoys crocheting, sewing, playing electric organ, photography, camping, traveling, computer (at age 70) and music. Her abiding interest and pride is her sons and their families, her friends, her Church, and her faith in God.

—submitted by Lois Jackson

Wood Family

Albert Hale Wood Senior was my great-great-grandfather. He came west in the 1850s, leaving his home in Plainfield, Connecticut, with his second wife, Julia Ann Williams Wood (1823–1899), their young son, Frederick Laureston Wood, and the six children by his first wife, Louisa Ann Burlingame Wood, who had died of consumption in 1847 in Connecticut. The family had stopped for a while in Akron, Ohio, where Frederick's younger brother, Albert Hale Wood Jr. (1855–1913), was born. The 1860 Census shows the six children from Louisa as Maria, James Asa, Clarinda, Zelotes, Jared and Ellen, ranging in ages from 17 to 25. Julia's Frederick was ten years old and Albert was age four.

During this time, my great-great-grandfather traveled further west, and finding to his liking 800 acres of farmland in Atkinson, Illinois along the Green River, he purchased same in late 1859.

Albert and Julia and their family settled in Geneseo, Illinois, where Albert was a businessman with many interests in addition to the farm. He had been a storekeeper and also a station master back east. Albert and Julia were both born in the little town of Foster, Rhode Island.

Late in December of 1860 another little family came west, from Belchertown in Massachusetts: Rufus Dunbar, his wife Lois Thurston Cook Dunbar, their daughter, Nellie, and their four sons, Franklin, Charles, Ernest, and William. Rufus and Lois bought land from Albert Wood, part of the parcel along the Green River.

In 1865 a daughter was born to Albert and Julia, at their home in Geneseo, and they named her Irene. Albert died in Geneseo in 1882, and was taken home to Foster, Rhode Island, where he is buried in the old Line Cemetery beside his first wife, Louisa, and his mother and father. Julia lived on until 1899 and is buried with most of her children in Chippiannock Cemetery.

Frederick, their eldest son, married Nellie M. Dunbar in Rock Island in 1875, and when Nellie died in 1878 they were living in Whitfield, Marshall County, Illinois.

Albert Wood Jr., a machinist, married Carrie R. Hagerty (1863–1749) in Rock Island about 1882, and is buried in Chippiannock beside his mother, Julia Ann Williams Wood, his wife, Carrie, his sister Irene Wood (1865–1890), and his three children, Lotie R. Wood (1884–1938), Grace B. Wood (1887–1942) and Richard A. Wood (1889–1970). Albert Junior's line appears to have died out, and his sister Irene never married.

Frederick and Nellie, however, had two sons, Herbert Arthur Wood and Edward Wood, and they have many descendants. Nellie died four months after giving birth to Edward, and she made a dying request that he be adopted by Georg and Karolina Mattern, a kindly, childless neighbor couple who had been caring for Nellie and Edward. Nellie was only 22 years old when she died. After the adoption, Frederick went west with the great threshing machines that were cultivating and harvesting the prairie, settling in Parkston, South Dakota, where he married again, and had one daughter, whom he named Irene after his little sister. Irene married and had numerous descendants.

Frederick opened a blacksmith and machinist shop in Parkston, and was building custom automobiles by 1900. He died in 1913 and is buried in the Dakota Cemetery in Parkston.

Herbert lived most of his life in Henry County, marrying Maude Smith and having two sons, Neuman and Lyle, and a daughter, Eva; there are numerous descendants. Edward stayed in Marshall County, marrying a local girl, Anna Katherine Troendly, and becoming a well-known taxidermist. Edward and Anna had twelve children!

It seems that Frederick never saw his children again after Nellie's death, and regretted the adoption till his dying day. In his last year he made contact with Edward and many photos were exchanged between the two.

Great-great Grandmother Julia Ann Williams Wood's grave had been lost to her descendants for more than a hundred years. Her family lay in unmarked graves in Chippiannock Cemetery. Most of them had died at Albert Junior's home, 3057 Tenth Avenue, Rock Island, and the home is now the property of Augustana College. In 2004 the writer and his cousin, Mr. Thomas Bogner of Henry, Illinois, donated the granite memorial that now marks the family graves, making it possible for Julia's many descendants to find the place where they can honor their ancestress and pay due respect.

—submitted by James E. Wood-Mattern

Notables

—Bruce Walters

Felicia Buford
1854—1904

Chippiannock Cemetery opened on August 15, 1855, offering 800 lots on 60 acres. The first lot of this original tract went to James Monroe Buford and his brother, Thomas Jefferson Buford. Felicia Buford, wife of James, died in 1904 at the age of 70. She was buried in that first lot, and was joined there the following year by her husband.

Felicia Julian Clarke, the youngest daughter of Joseph Clark, Esq., was married to James Monroe Buford in Kentucky on October 9, 1856. The bride was 22 years of age and the groom was 24. Her husband's family had already left the civilized, southern climate for northern Indian territory in 1838, so after the wedding, the newlyweds joined them in Rock Island.

The family did well for themselves in this growing community. James was one of the organizers of the First National Bank, served as president and secretary-treasurer of the Rock Island Plow Company, and sat on the board of directors of the Moline and Rock Island Horse Railway Company. At his death, he was still serving as president of the Rock Island Savings Bank.

The Buford family was also involved in local politics. Felicia's father-in-law had once been postmaster; her husband served a one-year term as mayor of Rock Island, twelve years as city treasurer, and was also president of the school board.

Felicia took on the job of running the household, directing the servants, entertaining business guests and ladies from the community. She also gave birth to four children: Herndon, who died at two years of age; Jane Swigert, her only daughter; James M., who died three months after his birth; and Clark Howe, who lived to age 22.

The Civil War was hard on the Buford family. Although they had ties to the south, they had lived in the north for more than two decades. Her husband James did not serve, but Felicia's two brothers-in-law did enlist. Napoleon Bonaparte Buford graduated from West Point and quickly rose through the ranks of the Union Army, mustering out as a Major-General.

John Buford, Jr. also graduated from West Point, starting the war as a second lieutenant. He was wounded in the second battle of Manassas, acted as chief of cavalry in the Potomac campaign, served on General McClellan's staff, and was appointed Major-General of Volunteers. John selected the site and opened the battle of Gettysburg, being the first Union leader to learn that General Lee's army was amassed there. He died of typhoid fever during the war, and was buried at West Point, where a monument is erected to his memory.

As proud as they were of these heroics, the Buford's in Rock Island were saddened by the conditions at the confederate prisoner of war camp on Rock Island Arsenal, and eased the prisoners' suffering by bringing them blankets and food.

In 1880, Felicia celebrated at the wedding of her daughter, Jane, who married Ransom Cable, thus joining two of the city's most powerful families. This was Ransom's second marriage, and Jane became the step-mother of two girls and two boys. Later that year, Felicia's daughter and son-in-law moved into a grand mansion on Second Avenue.

Jane was elected to serve on the Board of Directors of Chippiannock in 1896. Although women of that era weren't normally elected to such positions, the charter specified that vacancies in the Board were to be filled exclusively by the founders and their descendents. Her father's post on the board was vacated that year when he was elected Secretary, a position he filled until his death in 1906.

Napoleon Bonaparte Buford
1807–1883

In his 76 years, Napoleon Bonaparte Buford was a war hero, a surveyor, a business owner, a stockholder, a town founder, and one of the 14 men who incorprated Chippiannock Cemetery.

Born in 1807 to John Buford, Sr. and Nancy Hickman, Napoleon was named after the great Corsican general who was reigning as Emperor of France at that time. He was eighth in descent from Richard Beauford who came to Virginia from England in 1635.

Young N.B. graduated sixth in his class from West Point, studied law at Harvard, served as Assistant Professor of Natural and Experimental Philosophy at West Point, was appointed Civil Engineer of the State of Kentucky, and became a Topographical Engineer, all while still in his 20s.

Buford's first look at Rock Island was in 1828, when he was hired by the Army Corps of Engineers to survey the rapids on the Mississippi River. His ensuing report gave a general description of the Des Moines rapids (near Keokuk) and the Rock rapids (near Rock Island); detailed obstructions to navigation; discussed the practicability of locating a canal on either bank of the river or of deepening the channel of the river; showing the commercial advantages of making the Mississippi River more navigable; and finally estimating costs of his plans at $154,000. Later that year a fellow West Point graduate, Robert E. Lee, surveyed the same area with concurring results.

Impressed with Rock Island's location, N.B. urged his family to move from Kentucky to the land of opportunity. In 1936, his father and step-mother, Anne Bannister Watson, moved to Illinois with their three young sons—John Jr., Thomas Jefferson, and James Monroe. His father had served in the Kentucky Legislature and upon moving to Illinois, was elected to serve for four years as state senator.

Buford joined them in 1843, bringing with him his wife Sarah Childs and their son, Temple. There, he began an illustrious career as one of the town's leading capitalists. He ran the Iron and Grocery Store with his son; served as the secretary of the Rock Island & LaSalle railroad before becoming president of the Rock Island & Peoria Railroad and the Rock Island Gas, Light, & Coke Company; was part owner of the Coal Valley Mining Company and Rock Island Foundry & Machine Shop; and founded the town of Andalusia.

During this heyday, he built a gorgeous mansion for his second wife, Mary Ann Greenwood Pierce. The home was constructed in 1849 of brick shipped up from New Orleans by steamboat. It had seven bedrooms, two parlors, six fireplaces, a library, hand-carved paneling and doors, and two gold-plated chandeliers imported from France. The home also boasted many modern conveniences such as an ice house and two built-in brick ovens. Mary Ann didn't like it.

Unfortunately, his bank had invested heavily in the bonds of the Southern states, and the outbreak of the Civil War ruined him financially. Turning over all his property to his creditors, he helped form the 27th Illinois Volunteers and was commissioned colonel of the regiment. Buford proved to be an outstanding leader, taking part in a number of major sieges and battles.

In the spring of 1862, the Colonel joined Professor Steiner in a hot air balloon reconnaissance from his headquarters in Columbus, Kentucky. In previous wars, generals and staff officers scouted enemy troop movements from hilltops or mountains, sometimes resorting to climbing trees. This was the first war in which such surveys could be made from the air.

In April he was promoted to brigadier-general and was presented with a gift of sword, sword belt, sash, epaulettes, field glasses and spurs by his officers and men. Later in 1862 Buford suffered sunstroke and was sent to Washington D.C. While there, he wrote two letters to President Lincoln proposing a plan for the colonization of the west coast of Africa for the freed slaves. That year he was promoted to major-general.

Upon his recovery, he reported at Vicksburg during the siege, but was soon ordered to Illinois. There, he established a war orphan asylum, an industrial school for newly-liberated slaves, and prosecuted smugglers and other treasonous northerners who were trading with the enemy. He also organized more than 10,000 black men, some to serve as soldiers and others as self-supporting agriculturists. His troops continued to make raids into Mississippi and Arkansas, taking many prisoners of war. In 1865, he was promoted to brevet major-general for gallant and meritorious service.

After the war, Buford served as superintendent of the Federal Union Mining Company in Colorado, special Commissioner of Indian Affairs, and special commissioner and inspector for the railroads. He died in 1883, a resident of Chicago, after a long and distinguished career that spanned many decades and many vocations.

Although there were once over 80 Bufords living in Rock Island, there is not a single Buford relative here now.

Jonah H. Case
1797–1864

Jonah H. Case was one of the civic leaders who attended the first meeting of the founders of Chippiannock Cemetery in April 1855, along with Samuel Guyer, George Pleasants, Holmes Hakes, Marcus Osborn, Isaac Negus, George Bromley, H.A. Porter, Ebinezer Lathrop, C.M. Osborn, Miles Conway, William Lee, Ben Harper, and John Bean.

Jonah Case was born in Addison, Vermont, on April 15, 1797, and worked on the family farm for many years. In 1826, his family, including father Louden Sr., sister Jane, brothers Louden Jr. and Charles, moved to Morgan County, Illinois. Along with fellow Vermonter John W. Spencer, John's wife Louisa, and their son John, the family farmed the land for two years before traveling on to Rock Island. There the pioneer families settled on the north shore of the Rock River in the Indian village of Saukenuk, residing in the large wickiup of Sauk warrior

Black Hawk. They thought it was abandoned, but in early summer, Black Hawk returned from his winter traveling and found them there. The group moved out, building their own dwellings nearby.

His sister Jane married William Brashar and in 1829 gave birth to William, the first white child born on the mainland of Rock Island County.

Jonah married Julia Spencer, the sister of his friend John, who would become the first judge of the Rock Island County Court. Shortly after the marriage, the brothers–in–law laid out a 40–acre tract of land that ran from the Mississippi River up to what is now Eight Avenue, stretching between Seventeenth Street and Twenty–third Street.

Later, Jonah purchased 320 acres near Black Hawk's Spring. Mrs. Case used that spring as a source of household water and was upset whenever she found it muddied. One summer morning she got up very early to investigate and discovered Indian mothers using the spring to bathe their children, as they had probably been doing long before the whites had settled on their lands.

In 1833, Jonah was granted a license to keep a tavern after paying $5 tax and securing a bond. He wasn't allowed to set his own prices, however, as Rock Island County set fixed rates for tavern keepers. Meals were 37½ cents; half-pints of brandy and gin were 50 cents; quarts of cider and ale were 25 cents; lodging was 25 cents per person; and feed for horses was 75 cents.

Two years later, Case and Antoine LeClaire were granted a license to operate the first ferry across the Mississippi River just below Fort Armstrong. They charged rates 50–100% higher than the rates then being charged for the Rock River ferry.

In 1836, the Spencer-Case Addition was platted, including a block reserved exclusively for churches. The Methodists were allowed to build their church on one corner, the Baptists on a second, and Presbyterians on a third. The fourth corner was kept for whichever denomination was established next in the town. A brick schoolhouse was built in the center of the square.

Eventually the only two buildings that were actually erected there were vacated and in 1855 that section was donated by the two men to the city. After years of disuse, it was made into a fine plaza named Spencer Square. By 1868, that Square had become a squalid bog which was renovated in 1889 by the Park Commissioner into a grand plaza with a fountain and numerous statues. As the demographics of the city changed, the square was once again abandoned, and is currently the site of the Federal Building and Post Office.

Case was the manufacturer of the first plows in Rock Island County. He created these useful farm implements by strapping steel imported from England to wooden board plows. Later, Rock Island settlers Charles Buford, John Deere, and J.I. Case (no relation to Jonah) would develop the plow business into huge industrial empires.

Shifting his interest to brick-making, Jonah started a brickyard business. The first courthouse in Rock Island County was built in 1836 with 200,000 bricks furnished by Case at the cost of $8.00 per thousand. That building was demolished in 1897.

From October 1840 to February 1847, the *Upper Mississippian* was the leading newspaper in Rock Island. Case purchased the paper in January 1847, but the last issue came out on February 23 of that year.

His daughter Eliza married Kentucky native Roswell Richmond in 1855, and Jonah immediately put his new son-in-law in charge of one of his many brickyards.

Jonah Case died in 1864 at the age of 67. His wife died two years later.

Bailey Davenport
1823–1890

In 1855, Bailey Davenport and Mayor Ben Harper organized community leaders to form a cemetery, because the town had grown to the point that it was no longer desirable to bury the dead in Bailey's pasture, usually without any type of marker or record.

Bailey's father, George Davenport, was born in England in 1783, and was the area's first European settler, as well as one of its most successful, influential, and colorful pioneers. In 1816, Davenport arrived at Fort Armstrong (now Arsenal Island) as food contractor for the U.S. government. He supplied the troops and traded up and down the Mississippi River with the local Indian tribes.

Bailey was born September 15, 1823, near Cincinnati, Ohio, but grew up on Rock Island. The following year, George and his partner Russel Farnham erected the first building on the mainland, which served as a trading post, tavern, ferry and stagecoach station.

Shortly after the Black Hawk war in 1831, the Colonel withdrew from the Indian trade and devoted his time to developing lands on both sides of the Mississippi River. The area to the west became Davenport, Iowa, and the area to the east was named, eventually, Rock Island, Illinois.

The Davenport family remained friendly with the neighboring Indian tribes—the Sauk, Mesquakie, Winnebago—and was well-educated in their customs and attitudes. David Sears, son of an early settler, described Bailey as, "a peculiar man," who exhibited traits similar to the Indians he had befriended, wariness and suspicion among them.

In spite of, or maybe because of these characteristics, Bailey went on to become the most prosperous business leader early in Rock Island's history. He owned large tracts of land in Illinois, Iowa, Missouri, and Nebraska. He owned a thousand-acre homestead in Rock Island where he built a 40-room mansion, grazed cattle and thoroughbred horses, and provided a playing field for the baseball team, the Wapellos, who once defeated the Davenport, Iowa, team by a score of 118–27.

In addition, Bailey developed a coal mine at Black Hawk's Watch Tower and was the owner and manager of the Rock Island and Milan Steam and Horse Railway Company, which was used to transport the coal. After he beautified the area with a pavilion and walking trails, the trolley line transported visitors to his Watch Tower Park, situated on the bluffs overlooking the Rock River. Later he served as president of Peoples National Bank and was elected to serve five one-year terms as Mayor.

By the start of the Civil War, most of the Indians had left the area, and so had the troops. Without a purpose, Fort Armstrong was laid to ruin. As Confederate soldiers were being taken prisoner along the Mississippi River, flimsy barracks were constructed on the north shore of the island, using the deceased Colonel's home as headquarters.

At the same time, the federal armory at Harper's Ferry, Virginia, was continually being raided by Confederate troops and Congress began to look to the west for a safer location. Mayor Davenport, along with city council members from Rock Island, Moline, and Davenport, lobbied Congress to relocate the arsenal to the island where Fort Armstrong had once stood. To promote trade, he also donated land for a bridge that would connect the island to the mainland.

Bailey's personal life was as multi-faceted as his business holdings. His mother, Susan, was his step-sister, the daughter of the Colonel's wife Margaret. The Colonel fathered numerous other children whose mothers were the family servants and some Indian women from Tama.

One of Bailey's half-sisters was Elizabeth, the daughter of their white laundress. Lizzie and her husband, Niclos Ferkel, lived and farmed on land owned by Bailey near Illinois City. There they raised their 14 children, two of whom were named Bailey Davenport Ferkel and George Ferkel. Although he was a wealthy man, Bailey would argue with her when she purchased stoves and other household items in Rock Island, charging them to his accounts.

Bailey's father also had a daughter, Matilda, with one of his black servants. Matilda later gave birth to a son, Joe, fathered, it was said, by Bailey. According to Claus Lamp, the hired man who worked for Bailey for 24 years, Joe was very light-skinned and lived at Bailey's house for years. He went on to marry and have four children.

Bailey's house was built large enough for two families. He stored wood and coal in part of the house, and lived in the other half, entertaining many guests. His mother lived with him for years, as did Joe. He was often visited by numerous relatives of his mother and by Indians he had remained friends with.

Bailey Davenport died a bachelor in 1890.

Susan Lewis Goldsmith
1801–1878

When the founders of the Rock Island cemetery were deciding upon a name, Susan Goldsmith suggested Chip–pi–an–nock, *a Mesquakie word meaning "village of the dead." The Indians called this spot Manitou Ridge, believing that "the Great Spirit Manitou, who lived in the cave on the big island (Arsenal) flew over on the wings of a white swan, leaving in his wake a protective barrier of ice to hold back the flood waters of the Senisepo (Rock) and Sinnissippi (Mississippi) rivers."*

Susan Lewis was born on February 10, 1801, in Erie, Pennsylvania. Her mother, Margaret Bowling Lewis was a widow living in St. Louis when she married George Davenport. He settled his new family at Fort Armstrong on an island in the midst of Indian territory in 1816. Susan was 15 years old.

The following year Susan gave birth to George L. Davenport, named after his father. He was the first white child born in the territory. Seven years later she bore another Davenport son and named him Bailey. For many years, the nearest white families could only be found in St. Louis, Chicago, or Prairie du Chien. She became well acquainted with the Indians who lived and traded in the area. The journals she kept reflect many incidents and events about the Sauk, Mesquakie, and Winnegabo. Her son George L. was embraced by the Mesquakie; and Susan also spoke their language and knew their customs.

Around 1826, she married a man named Goodale, and in 1849, she was wed to Rev. Zachariah Goldsmith, an Episcopalian minister who did not treat her well. She inherited a life estate on the island at the death of Col. Davenport and remained there until 1856 when she bought her own home in Rock Island. Her son Bailey resided with her until he built his own 40-room mansion six years later.

Susan's other son George L. married, had children, and moved to the other side of the Mississippi River. He did not fare as well as his brother and died a poor man, even though he was better educated. While his estate, and his debts, were tied up in court, his daughters continued to live in the big brick house with the windows nailed shut. Bailey's hired man Claus Lamp would often cross the river to pick them up in the family carriage and take them to visit their grandmother and uncle.

Mrs. Goldsmith, her son Bailey, and two other Episcopalians built the Rock Island Episcopal Church, which includes a memorial window for Susan, who died in 1878 at Bailey's home. The church continued to receive her financial support from a trust fund she established.

According to one of Claus Lamp's daughters who worked for Bailey, Mrs. Goldsmith was a good woman to work for. She was a quiet, reserved woman, who was generous with the poor. Everyone called her "Missus." Upon her death, though, her marker reads Mother, as does Margaret's marker. Her August 5, 1878, *Argus* obituary reflects the social courtesy of the times, skirting her complex familial ties and focusing instead on her earnest and cheerful character and her benevolent nature.

Samuel S. Guyer
1814–1883

Judge Samuel Guyer was one of Chippiannock Cemetery's founding members, serving as Chairman at the original meeting, and serving as vice president of the Board from 1875 until his death in 1883.

Samuel Guyer was born on December 26, 1814, in Lewistown, Pennsylvania, where he became a contractor and worked on the construction of the Pennsylvania Canal aqueduct. Upon its completion, he switched gears and took a job at the *Harrisburg Chronicle* as a reporter, where his older brother served as editor–in–chief.

In 1839, Samuel accompanied his mother and sisters to Peoria, Illinois, where he started a trade of building flatboats. He stocked his boats with goods and made frequent selling excursions downriver to Natchez and New Orleans. When a tornado blew through Natchez in 1842, he lost everything he owned. The gale winds were so fierce, even the clothing he wore was stripped from his body, and he was blown into the river.

Upon returning to Peoria, Guyer began the study of law with Mr. Knowlton. The following year, he traveled with his brother to Rock Island with all of $7.00 in his pockets. In 1847, he was elected sheriff of Rock Island County. That same year Samuel married Annette Holmes, the daughter of Judge George Holmes from Port Byron. The couple had one son and one daughter.

During his campaigning, Guyer would go to a harvest field and work all day, often competing against the best worker in the field. If he won, the agreement was that all field hands present would vote for him on election day.

Guyer served his second term as sheriff beginning in 1849, then turned his interest to mining development. He was one of the original owners of the Coal Valley Mining Company and the Rock Island & Peoria Railway. He and his partners sold their shares in 1861, and he became associated with Hakes, Guyer & Company, which built the Rock Island Paper Mill along the Mississippi River just below Weyerhaeuser & Denkmann's saw mill.

Samuel was one of the city leaders who attended that first cemetery association assembly in April 1855. Over the next 18 months by–laws, rules, and restrictions were agreed upon in subsequent meetings. In February, 1857, Samuel was sent by the committee to Springfield, the capitol of Illinois, to expedite their application for a perpetual charter.

When Probate Court Judge John Wilson passed away in 1871, Guyer was appointed by the Republican Convention to finish the term. He was elected in 1873 to serve a full four-year term.

Samuel Guyer died in 1883, survived by his wife Annette, daughter Nettie, and son Edward. Pursuant to the cemetery bylaws, Edward, who was born the year the cemetery was founded, was appointed to serve on the Chippiannock Board of Directors upon his father's death. He was elected president in 1887 and served in that capacity for 50 years.

Holmes Hakes
1818–1900

Holmes Hakes served as one of the first directors on the board of the newly–organized Chippiannock Cemetery in 1855, purchased one of the first 11 tracts sold there, and served as its president from 1866 to 1883.

Holmes Hakes was born in 1819 in Oneida County, New York. When he was 22 years old, he married Almeda Riggs, a Kentucky native who was age 18. Their eldest son George was born October 10, 1844, in Liberty, Missouri. Three years later the family moved to Rock Island County, Illinois, at the height of the industrial revolution.

In 1841, the town had been called Stephenson, but was changed to Rock Island by the Illinois State legislature. In 1847, only a year after settling there, Hakes was elected to serve as one of the original Trustees of the Village of Rock Island. A committee, made up of Hakes, Napoleon Bonaparte Buford, and James Hadsell, was appointed to draft the city charter.

The committee located the city charter of Quincy, Illinois, and rewrote it, substituting the words "Rock Island" wherever "Quincy" appeared in the document, and altering the description of the city's location. In 1849, the charter was accepted and Benjamin Barrett was elected Mayor.

Besides serving his community, Hakes stayed busy running his two diverse businesses—a jewelry store and a nursery. He once placed this notice in the newspaper regarding new wares:

"Hakes has arrived home from the east with a superb lot of jewelry, clocks, watches, etc, including many other fancy affairs which we haven't had time to look over. Read his advertisement and call and see his Shanghai chickens, which are big enough to look over you. After that you will no doubt find the first convenient door a good place to drop into to hide your littleness. You will most likely find Mr. H. at home, there, and can talk to him at your leisure."

He took on W.L. Riggs as his partner in the jewelry store in 1854. Nine years later they moved the store to Davenport, Iowa.

In 1856, Holmes, along with Samuel Guyer and Napoleon Buford, his co-committee members on the city and cemetery boards, formed the Coal Valley Mining Company. In the next decade, he bought and sold numerous buildings and plots of land. Empire Block, a three-story brick building, contained a store owned by Hakes, where he and A.K. Philleo sold groceries and provisions. He also owned the building that housed the broom factory operated by Jacob Kuhn, and lots of 15 and 30 acres near the town of Camden Mills.

From the proceeds of these sales, he opened a company called Holmes Hakes and Son, paper dealers. In 1872, he and George De Land started a large paper mill in Milan, which they sold three years later to the Rock River Paper Company. At the time of the sale, Hakes' mill employed 35–40 men and produced five to six tons of wrapping paper per day.

By 1888, Hakes had become physically and mentally weakened, and moved to Fresno, California, with his wife, a grandson, and two hired men. In 1900 his daughter was appointed to be his legal guardian. One day while taking a walk along an irrigation ditch, he had another of his fainting spells and died there at the age of 81. His daughter transported his body back to Rock Island so he could be buried alongside the other men who helped develop this area from pioneer frontier into a bustling city.

Ben Harper
1817–1887

Mayor Ben Harper was one of the leading citizens of Rock Island who gathered to form Chippiannock Cemetery.

Ben Harper was born in the City of Brotherly Love in 1817, and brought that feeling of community spirit west with him. At age 14, he left Philadelphia for Cincinnati to become a wagon maker. His father had a cellar full of cider which he couldn't sell, so he gave it to his son. The enterprising young man built a flatboat and transported that cider to St. Louis, where he traded it for dry goods. Traveling back up the Ohio River with the merchandise, he established a store in Ohio.

In 1850, Ben sold his interest in the store and arrived in Rock Island with $75,000 and a dream to turn the town with a population of less than 2,000 into a bustling metropolis. A decade later, Rock Island was home to 10,000 people and dozens of booming industries.

Harper contributed to this growth through many ventures, including the Coal Valley mines, the Rock Island Gas Works, and the Rock Island & Moline Horse Railway Company.

Just five years after arriving in Rock Island, he was elected mayor. During his one-year tenure, he paved four blocks on the levee, completed a sidewalk and road-grading project, increased the police force, provided for additional firefighting equipment, established a policy forbidding wooden buildings downtown, negotiated for the quit claim deeds to Spencer Square, led a tree-planting campaign, built Rock Island's first hospital, established a pauper's burial ground, and started a city market house.

Also during his year as mayor, Harper attended a meeting in the First Presbyterian Church to discuss the organization of the Rock Island Library and Reading Association. A month later it was a reality with a librarian and 1,000 volumes.

Some of these deeds he accomplished by raising money from the wealthy citizens, but most of it came in the form of taxes. A grocer's license to sell goods (and liquor), was raised to $200 per year; steamboats paid $1.00 each time they docked at the city wharf; vendors selling coal, wood, and hay on the levee were charged $8 per month for a 30'x50' space. He also established a policy of "strict economy and rigid accountability" from all city officials.

In 1868, Ben purchased the Island City Hotel, enlarging it to four stories and improving the brick structure by adding a mansard roof. He renamed the establishment the Rodman House, in honor of General Thomas J. Rodman, commandant of Rock Island Arsenal, Ben's friend and the inventor of the Rodman gun and shells. As the finishing touches were being put on the décor, a fire broke out, reducing the Rodman House to ashes and scorched bricks.

A year later, Ben built Harper House on the same spot. He intended the new hotel to be a "monument to Rock Island, a show place which will make visitors realize that we have enterprise here and faith in the future." The elegant establishment boasted 14 mirrors paneling the walls of the banquet hall and was the first hotel in the west to provide fire escapes.

On February 21, 1871, a grand opening banquet was held, attended by 800 members of Rock Island society and distinguished out–of–town visitors. Recognizing that the hotel was "a quarter of a century ahead of the town," the citizens presented Ben with gifts of a $1,000 piano and a $300 silver pitcher. Reporters from as far away as Chicago and St. Louis were there to get the story for their newspapers.

A few years later, he constructed Harper Opera House, a three–story building that offered store–fronts on the ground floor, with the remainder being used for the opera house. It was a grand affair with a large stage, gas lighting, steam heat, 540 upholstered seats, and 311 other seats. Many famous celebrities graced its stage, including Lily Langtry, Buffalo Bill Cody, Tom Thumb, Sarah Bernhardt, and General W.T. Sherman.

Ben's son, Stuart, married Grace Velie, daughter of Stephen Velie and granddaughter of John Deere. Ben Harper died in 1887 at the age of 70, leaving a city much bigger and better than the frontier town he had settled in 37 years earlier.

Charles Bishop Knox
1818–1890

The first undertaker in Rock Island County, Charles Knox made the coffins and provided funeral services for residents buried at Chippiannock Cemetery.

Although he was born in Hampden County, Massachusetts, on June 27, 1818, Charles Knox came to be a pioneer and beloved community leader in Rock Island County. At age 16, Charles moved to Ellington County, Mass., to apprentice as a cabinet maker. His employer died three years later, so he was forced to move to Pittsfield, Mass., to complete his training. He worked as a cabinet maker in Springfield, Mass., for two years before moving west to Rock Island and making a name for himself.

Charles was married to Mary Gorham, who was born on September 14, 1819, and died April 20, 1893.

Knox immediately opened a furniture shop upon arriving in Rock Island. In 1841, there was no such job as undertaker, so cabinet makers often developed a sideline building coffins. Because these were made to order, Knox was often awakened late at night to make a coffin, sometimes for a deceased person living a long distance from the city.

As for funerals, friends and family of the deceased would need to volunteer to be sure the service ran smoothly. This sometimes included nailing pine boards together for a coffin, greeting mourners, and organizing the itinerary. People who had few relatives, or whose families were too bereft or disorganized to provide such services did not receive the dignified solemnities they deserved.

In 1852, Knox began the vocation of undertaking by conducting the funeral services as well as making the coffins. He was the first person to do so in this part of the country. During the Civil War, he was responsible for making coffins and burying the two thousand confederate prisoners who died on Arsenal Island, which averages out to nearly 500 coffins per year.

Charles served his community in many other ways, as well. He was elected to the first Board of Alderman of the City of Rock Island, served as Supervisor for two years, acted as Coroner for eight years, and held the post of Chief of the Fire Department for many years. In addition, he was also a devoted member of the Odd Fellows and Druids Societies, and a staunch family man.

Twenty years after starting the undertaking business, Charles was joined by his son B. Frank Knox, who served as Rock Island City Alderman as had his father. Charles also had three other sons: Edwin B. Knox, who served as mayor of Moline before becoming a guard at Rock Island Arsenal; Samuel P. Knox, another Alderman in Rock Island; and Carter B. Knox.

One month shy of his 72nd birthday, Charles Knox passed away after suffering kidney and liver afflictions for the previous six months. His son Frank carried on the family business until his death in 1914, when the business then passed to Frank's son, Harry T. Knox.

Isaac Negus
1799–1883

Isaac Negus attended the first meeting of the founders of Chippiannock Cemetery in April, 1855, and was elected to the Board in 1866.

Isaac was one of Rock Island's pioneer citizens. He was born in Fabius, New York, on December 31, 1799, and lived with his parents and eight siblings while attending school. When he turned 21, he left the family farm to drive a team that towed barges on the Erie Canal. He and his horses received a total pay of $1.00 per day.

Eventually the young man left the manual labor behind and began to sell quality clocks. He then traveled to southern Illinois, where he settled in Edwardsville in 1829. Isaac moved north to Chicago and became a contractor on the Illinois and Michigan canal, supervising a large work force there for four years.

On October 8, 1844, Negus arrived in Rock Island to pursue a career in merchandising.

By the time he arrived in Rock Island County, he had a third wife, Jerusha Waldo, who had married him on November 28, 1839. They had three children, Anna, William, and Charles.

Eight years after his arrival, Isaac became a member of the banking firm of Mann, Negus and Lee. After it dissolved he gave up on running a business and turned his efforts toward real estate.

In anticipation of the arrival of the Chicago, Rock Island & Pacific Railroad, the first train to connect Rock Island with the east coast, the leading moguls of Rock Island planned for a celebration. Isaac served on the Committee of Reception that planned the festive occasion held on February 22, 1854. When seven steamboats left the shores of the town five months later, filled to capacity with dignitaries and newspaper editors from all across the country, Isaac Negus was one of the privileged locals who participated in the Grand Excursion that traveled up to St. Anthony Falls, Minnesota.

On August 18, 1863, Isaac ran an advertisement in the newspaper stating:

> I will pay the highest price, in "Green Backs"
> for 100 Cavalry Horses —
> to be delivered immediately.

In 1875, he purchased The Rock Island House for the sum of $12,000, much to the delight of the townspeople. This hotel had been built in 1843 to serve as a stagecoach stop, but had fallen into dilapidation. He tore down the existing structure and rebuilt it as a fine establishment. He also built a home for his family at 1229 Second Avenue that he named Negus Flats; a block of houses at 1301–1307 Second Avenue, which he called Negus Row Houses; and Negus Hall on Seventeenth Street. He also owned a building on Market Square.

In 1880, Negus became weakened and was near death a number of times. Three years later, at the age of 83, Isaac passed away, leaving an estate estimated at $200,000. He was survived by his three children. His wife, Jerusha, had died ten years earlier.

Marcus Brutus Osborn
1803–1898

When Chippiannock Cemetery was organized, county pioneer Marcus Osborn was one of 11 original buyers of plots.

Marcus Brutus was born in Troy, New York, in 1803. He attended school with Sidney Breese, who served on the Illinois Supreme Court from 1857–1878, sitting as Chief Justice for five of those years. Marcus then taught school in Connecticut, where one of his pupils was Morrison Waite, who later was appointed Chief Justice of the United States Supreme Court and served from 1874–1888.

Marcus served as city clerk in Richmond, Virginia, in 1818 and was married in Ithaca, New York. He engaged in the lumber and whaling business until his family moved to Henry County, Illinois, where he served as county commissioner. After settling in Rock Island, he became active in the business and public affairs of his new home.

Retaining his interest in education, he served as county school commissioner from 1850 to 1853. He used his influence to raise funds for the establishment of the pioneer institution Geneseo Seminary, and organized Rock Island University, which provided a higher education to local students from 1841 to 1844. In addition, he served for 34 years as a trustee of Knox College, a liberal arts school in Galesburg that was founded by abolitionists in 1837.

He was a founder of the Rock Island and Camden Plank Road Company, which did not thrive. He established a stock and real estate brokerage office that offered services related to taxes, deeds, fire and marine insurance, and all other business connected with land agency. He was also one of the founders of the Chicago & Rock Island Railroad Company, participating on the Committee of Reception for the Grand Arrival of the train on February 22, 1954.

Furthering his business ventures, Osborn co-founded one of the first banks in the county, The Rock Island Bank, serving as its president. On December 21, 1852, a notice appeared in the newspaper assuring the public that the checks of M.B. Osborn were wholly secured by pledge of public stocks and cash deposited with the bank, and that they would be promptly redeemed in coin at the Bank counter. This was a chaotic time for fledgling financial institutions, since wildcat currency—money issued without security by financially irresponsible banks—was all too common during that era. His bank closed its doors five years later in the Panic of 1857.

During the Civil War, Osborn was a U.S. Navy Paymaster, and during his first cruise in the Gulf of Mexico, served as volunteer Chaplain. Upon his return home he served as Postmaster from 1867 to 1871. In addition to supervising the mail carriers and overseeing operations, one of his duties was to publish notice in the newspaper each day describing mail routes and time of delivery, as well as listing unclaimed letters.

On February 22, 1866, the first annual meeting of the Old Settlers Association of Rock Island County convened at Babcock's Hall. Membership in this exclusive club was limited to the men and women who had moved to the area in 1846 or earlier. The all-day affair started at noon, with the Lead Mine Silver Band playing as members assembled. Speakers recalled the early days, gave orations, and offered toasts. A sumptuous banquet was served at 5:00 p.m., followed by more toasts, including a tribute to the memory of deceased pioneers, and a eulogy to George Washington by Osborn.

Marcus Osborn died at the age of 90 in May 1893 in Salt Lake City, where he had lived for 20 years due to failing health. He was returned to Chippiannock to be buried next to his wife, who died in 1875.

Morris Rosenfield
1842–1898

Fourteen years after the founding of Chippiannock Cemetery, Morris Rosenfield, along with three other local businessmen, co-founded the Hebrew Burying Ground Association.

Morris was one of the million German immigrants to emigrate to America in the 1850s. Born to Jacob and Ellen Ullmann Rosenfield in Wurtemberg on December 18, 1842, he arrived in his new country in 1854. Unlike many others, who settled in numerous places out east before finding their way to the Mississippi Valley, Morris came directly to Rock Island County and remained there his entire life.

Although his first business was in leather, in 1869 he founded the Moline Wagon Company with his partners

James First, a wheelwright who started repairing wagons in the 1850s, and C.A. Benson. Just three years later they incorporated their business with a capital of $100,000, naming Rosenfield as president and manager.

Being firmly established in his vocation, Rosenfield then traveled to Cincinnati, Ohio, and married Julia E. Ottenheimer, who was born in that state. They went on to have three children: Irene, Walter, and Charles.

When Rosenfield and his partners started out, they had small shops and little money, and were able to produce around 100 wagons per year. Morris proved to be a smart manger with good business acumen, and led the company in an extensive expansion. In 1881, he invested in Deere, Wells & Company, a sales branch of John Deere in Omaha, Nebraska, which prompted many Deere sales branches to sell the Moline wagon. Eventually, the Moline Wagon Company employed between 375 and 400 men, and had the capacity to manufacture 100 wooden wagons a day. In Moline, a city boasting many successful industries, the wagon company was one of the leading manufacturing firms.

In addition to running this large operation, Rosenfield sat on the Board of Directors of the First National Bank of Moline, and by 1893, was a wealthy man. That year he moved his family into a magnificent, Romanesque–style mansion that boasted eighteen rooms, seven fireplaces, and a third-floor ballroom, built at a cost of $50,000. This was quite an impressive number, considering most other homes in the city were built for $1,000 to $3,000 during that time.

Morris retired in 1896, handing the reins over to his son, Walter. Morris died two years later, and never knew that by 1909, more than one million Moline wagons were in use throughout the country. Walter sold the company in 1911 to Deere, who renamed it the John Deere Wagon Company. Two years later, the Moline factory became known as the Wagon Works, and all wagons made there displayed the John Deere logo on its wagon box and rear axle.

The Rosenfield mansion still stands. When Walter moved his family into the Charles Buford home in 1916, he sold the house to St. Joseph's, who used it as a convent for 37 years. It was then sold to the Tri–Cities Jewish Center and was used as an educational building until 1977. Today it serves as a senior citizen center adjacent to The Coventry, a 147–unit apartment building for seniors.

Leopold Simon
1855–1940

In 1869, Henry Burgower, Morris Rosenfield, Leopold Simon, and Joseph May founded the Hebrew Burying Ground Association. This one acre of land was laid out in Chippiannock Cemetery and enclosed with a hedge. Leopold Simon served as secretary of the organization.

Leopold Simon was born in Mannheim, Germany, in 1855 and immigrated to America as a young man. He was employed in a wholesale dry goods firm in Chicago for a few years before making his way west to Rock Island. On April 28, 1878, he married Miss Rebecca Mosenfelder. She was born in Philadelphia, moved to Rock Island with her parents, Mr. and Mrs. Julius Mosenfelder, and was educated in the Rock Island schools.

That same year, Leopold went into partnership with Alphons Mosenfelder, a relationship which lasted until

1904. Alphons then opened Mosenfelder & Sons, while Leopold and his new partner, Moritz Landauer, founded Simon & Landauer, a men's clothing store at Second and Harrison Streets in Davenport. In 1933, the store moved to a new location and a second store was opened in Rock Island.

Simon built a stately Free Classic Queen Anne home on Nineteenth Street for his family in 1885. One hundred and twenty years later, the house was still standing and showing off its fine original details.

Besides his clothing stores, Simon was interested in banking, and in 1890, was one of the founding directors of Rock Island Savings Bank. It was the first savings bank in the city and began with capital stock in the amount of $100,000.

On March 10, 1930, his wife Rebecca passed away. At the age of 84, Leopold Simon died on May 7, 1940, while residing in Huntington, West Virginia, with his daughter. He had been a leading business owner in the Davenport and Rock Island area for more than 50 years, and was remembered as one of the first merchants in the Midwest to use a one–price policy in his store.

Mary Hall Wadsworth
1841–1930

P.L. Mitchell was a charter member of the Chippiannock Cemetery Association and served as secretary from 1860 until his death in 1895. His son Phil then took his place until his death in 1906. That year, his daughter, Mary Wadsworth, was elected to the Board of Directors of Chippiannock, and was directly involved with the management of the organization.

Miss Mary Hall Mitchell was born to Catherine and Philemon Libby Mitchell in Georgetown, Kentucky, on August 4, 1841. Philemon was born in 1812 in Linington, Maine, to father Isaac Mitchell, who was also born in Maine, and mother Martha Libby, who had emigrated from Ireland with her parents. Mary had three sisters, Annie M., Kate M. and Laura M., and one brother, Phil. The children attended schools in Georgetown and Lexington,

Kentucky. In 1856, the family moved to Rock Island County, Illinois.

Mary's father was a banker in Kentucky, and after selling his interest, he and his partner Philander Cable brought $80,000 with them when they relocated their families to Rock Island. Upon leaving Kentucky, they freed their slaves, bringing along some who chose to remain with the family as paid servants. Jackson, their houseman, was reported to have varnished and painted the woodwork when the Mitchell home was built.

Two years before Mary's nuptials, her father and his partner opened the First National Bank of Rock Island, which was one of the original national banks put in operation in the United States. Mr. Mitchell went on to be involved in numerous other businesses, such as the Rock Island Savings Bank, R.I. Plow Works, R.I. Buggy Company, R.I. Children's Carriage Works, R.I. Stove Company, R.I. Glass Works, Davenport & Rock Island Street Railway System, and Chippiannock Cemetery.

Miss Mitchell married Henry T. Wadsworth in 1865. The wedding was held at her parents' grand home and was attended by 100 guests. The couple honeymooned in Kentucky, and upon their return, were honored at a reception attended by 200 guests from Rock Island and Davenport. Henry was a dry goods merchant in Rock Island, and his brother William, who married Mary's sister, Anne, had a similar establishment in Davenport.

Mary and Henry had no children, and eventually resided with her father. After Henry died in 1872, Mary continued to live in the Mitchell home. The beautiful house, built in Italianate architecture, had nine rooms plus servants' quarters over the kitchen, and was decorated with walnut woodwork. A parlor that ran the length of the house displayed twin "horn of plenty" Italian marble fireplaces and had 12½ foot ceilings. On one wall was attached a frieze of grey, cream and rose in alternating fruit and flower designs. It was installed by Mrs. Wadsworth after a trip to Europe, where she saw a similar frieze in a castle there. A 32 foot by 80 foot coach house which sat at the rear of the lot contained granaries, supply rooms, and two upper story hay rooms.

In 1895, Mary's father passed away and she inherited the family home, where she stayed busy running the household and entertaining guests. In April 1896, she donated the funds for a new Memorial Christian Church to be built in the memory of her father at a cost of $40,000. She was a Sunday school teacher there and for many years she served as Primary Superintendent of the Bible School. She was also involved in many other church activities and community charities. Her sisters and a nephew donated the pulpit, a large hall lamp, and a Kimball organ.

Mary and her siblings also presented the church with a memorial window on the north wall of the sanctuary in honor of their parents. The east wall now contains memorial windows for Mary and her sister Anne, who died in 1919. In September 2006, the Rock Island City Council overturned a recommendation from the Rock Island Preservation Commission to give landmark status to the church, thus putting its future into question.

In 1917, Mary sold the Mitchell home, which has been designated a historical landmark, and moved into an apartment in the Como Hotel. She died in December 1930 at the age of 89.

Mission Statement: To fund efforts and projects to preserve the cemetery as an historical venue and maintain its landscaping and historically significant monuments while it also serves the arts, education, science, and the general needs of the public in the present time.

For generations, Chippiannock has been famous for the design and artisitic improvement of its landscaping and monuments, many of them famous works of art. Through the years, it has also become a significant venue for artists, photographers, and lecturers, and we have stretched our physical and financial resources to accommodate their interests. This is how the cemetery became famous as a landmark enjoyed by Quad City citizens and visitors from all over the country. In fact, in 1994 Chipiannock was awarded a place in the National Register of Historic Places. That has been the happy result of all our efforts. All very well of course. Needless to say, there are special challenges in maintaining a landmark such as this one. Roads, trees, and shrubs need to be maintained. Many of them need replacement after so many years. And some of Chippiannock's priceless and venerable monuments need to be straightened and reset. This is costly maintenance.

In 1999, the Chippiannock Cemetery Heritage Foundation (CCHF) was formed to raise funds for the historical and preservation programs, newsletter, and educational outreach we have worked hard to provide through the years. The CCHF has the 501(c)(3) status with the IRS, and all contributions are tax deductible.

Currently the CCHF offers walking tours of history, Victorian symbolism, trees, and birds. Self-guided walking tour brochures are available at no cost. We also sponsor a genealogical workshop and other workshops of community interest. If you would like to receive our newsletter, please consider membership in the CCHF. Membership in the CCHF is $25 per year for an individual, and $45 per year for a family. Membership will include the newsletter and notification of discounts and special events. Please make your contribution or membership check to the CCHF and mail it to:

> **Chippiannock Cemetery Heritage Foundation**
> 2901 12th Street
> Rock Island, IL
> 61201-5335
> info@chippiannock.com

Printed in the United States
60793LVS00002B/172-333